LOVE @ FIRST CLICK

LOVE @ FIRST CLICK

THE ULTIMATE GUIDE TO ONLINE DATING

LAURIE DAVIS

ATRIA PAPERBACK

New York • London • Toronto • Sydney • New Delhi

ATRIA PAPERBACK
A Division of Simon & Schuster, Inc.
1230 Avenue of the Americas
New York, NY 10020

First Atria Paperback edition January 2013

ATRIA PAPERBACK and colophon are trademarks of
Simon & Schuster, Inc.

For information about special discounts for bulk purchases, please
contact Simon & Schuster Special Sales at 1-866-506-1949 or
business@simonandschuster.com.

The Simon & Schuster Speakers Bureau can bring authors to
your live event. For more information or to book an event,
contact the Simon & Schuster Speakers Bureau at 1-866-248-3049
or visit our website at www.simonspeakers.com.

Designed by Julie Schroeder

Manufactured in the United States of America

10 9 8 7 6 5 4 3 2 1

Library of Congress Cataloging-in-Publication Data

Davis, Laurie.
   Love @ first click : the ultimate guide to online dating /
Laurie Davis. — 1st Atria paperback ed.
      p. cm.
   1. Online dating. I. Title. II. Title: Love at first click.
   HQ801.82.D386 2013
   306.730285—dc23
                                    2012030198

ISBN 978-1-4516-8703-3
ISBN 978-1-4516-8704-0 (ebook)

For my mom, who always made sure
I knew the definition of love.

Contents

LOVE @ FIRST CLICK

Introduction

ONLINE DATING VIRGIN

While most people are settling into their offices at nine A.M., I'm doing a different kind of hustle: the Starbucks shuffle. Rushing through the doors of the coffee shop, I grab my grande skim chai latte from the barista and wave to Krissy, who's hunkered over her Mac at the corner table on the second floor.

As I ascend the stairs, gray stilettos click-clacking, a few heads turn. OK, I might be a *tad* overdressed for the plastic cup/green straw crowd. On the Upper West Side of Manhattan, mommies decked out in yoga pants rule the streets with their stroller brigade. Although my baby-blue chiffon dress is unquestionably subdued, the gold-sequin sheath underneath is certainly over the top. But I've learned that you can never be too careful when your day's agenda is as unpredictable as the Wall Street ticker. Today I'm meeting with my team and some clients at the coffice, then heading to a cocktail party later on. In between, who knows? It's possible I'll be called into a meeting with executives to consult on their latest technology development, meet with an ex-boyfriend-turned-client, or make an on-camera appearance for an early-evening talk show.

My iPhone trills in my handbag, and when I dig it out, the screen reveals a number I've never seen.

"Good morning, eFlirt Expert," I answer.

"Hi. I just came across your website and need some help. I've never online dated, and I don't even know where to start. I mean, what site should I join? What should I say in my profile? How do I know the guy I meet isn't a serial killer?" the caller asks. I can hear the confusion and desperation in her voice, and my brain kicks into customer-service gear.

"I can help you," I assure her. "Let's address sites first so you can log on and get dating right away. Tell me a bit about yourself."

As she fills me in on the inner workings of her life, likes, and loves, I consider her dating details, recommend that she join Match.com and HowAboutWe, and give her some safety precautions.

This conversation isn't an unusual way to start off the week. Monday is our highest-traffic day for online dating virgins. After a weekend of no dates (or dates gone wrong), emotions naturally run high—even when you're an otherwise level-headed executive, like this fabulous female.

Needless to say, I'm not your typical CEO. I popped my online dating cherry twelve years ago. Contrary to popular belief, I wasn't lurking on Match.com in 2001 because I was a desperate forty-five-year-old living in a basement apartment with only my *Star Wars* collection for company. Quite the opposite: I was a bouncy, fresh-faced nineteen-year-old who was addicted to technology and fully supportive of anything that could enhance my boy-crazy lifestyle.

Back in the day, online dating was my dirty little secret. The stigma meant that I couldn't blab to my girlfriends about my Yahoo! Personals encounters. One time, I slipped and told a girlfriend about my latest cyber-flirting fail, but instead of laughing at the expense of the guy who had made *me* chauffeur *him* to our date, I got an earful about how I could have been dragged into a dark alley. Thanks, Mom.

It was clear to me that being an early adopter in the preblog era meant devising my own rule book to handle precarious digital dating situations. Because let's face it, although I met some incredibly fabulous guys throughout my online dating journey, there were also those who left a *lot* to be desired. I tested different approaches and quickly figured out how to get anything I wanted online. Soon enough, I was having a blast weeding out the undesirables through nuances in their profiles, setting intentions that kept my mind-set in check, and perfecting the online lingo to generate dates.

Meanwhile, without any experience in production or marketing, I somehow landed a position as an associate producer at a digital marketing firm with a little bit of luck and an inside contact. While my friends were doing keg stands at frat parties and living out their final college years, I dropped out of music school and was flying by the seat of my Banana Republic trousers, sitting in on meetings with Fortune 500 CEOs, strategizing creative campaigns for product launches, and executing multimillion-dollar events.

As my career evolved, so did dating on the Web. The stigma was beginning to lift, and it was becoming more socially acceptable. So, I persuaded friends to opt in to online dating, too, and as a vet, I became their go-to for advice. Sprucing up friends' online dating lives became an entertaining diversion from my high-pressure nine-to-five.

Nine years after my first log-in, one of my friends called to gush that he was moving in with his girlfriend. And suddenly, I had my lightbulb moment. I realized that I had helped him meet her online! And he wasn't the only one. Smiling faces of other couples I'd introduced and singles I'd helped get laid flashed through my mind.

This was my hidden passion, the thing I took for granted all these years, the thing that made me most happy in life: helping people find love at first click.

Inspired, I started to research, create, and brand my business in my pajamas right from my couch. Forty-eight hours later, with fifty dollars and a Twitter account, my company went live, and I became the founder of eFlirt Expert, an online dating consultancy.

On my way to touching the techie lives of singles, many thought I was straitjacket-bound. As you can imagine, revealing that I was an online dating coach made for some, ahem, *interesting* dinner-party conversation. "Why would someone need an online dating coach?" their creased brows and snickers behind my back seemed to say. In fact, my then-boyfriend was one of the haters, so I ditched him.

But I knew my vision would be much-needed guidance for those wanting to power up their digi-date lives. Sure enough, two months later, my advice made its mass-media debut in the *Washington Post,* and years later, the company is thriving. My counsel has been featured in more than two hundred international media outlets. And in a world where everyone communicates as much via text message as we do through body language, my Certified eFlirters and I are the digital dating whisperers. Our clients DM us on Twitter when a flirt ends up failing, send along their latest email string disasters, and text us mid-date when things don't go as planned offline. We decode every tweet, ghostwrite every email, and save budding relationships from Facebook status disaster.

I've personally worked one-on-one with nearly a thousand singles all around the world, acting as their online dating ghostwriter, managing their eFlirting life, and coaching them through hookups and relationships. They've had fun and found partnerships, and many are married now (there are even some eFlirt babies). I've learned that there are few things more rewarding than helping people find love every day. Each time a client changes his or her relationship status on Facebook, I do a little dance. And secretly, I wake up every morning feeling like eCupid. Now, let me help you.

Online dating has evolved so dramatically since the first time I sent my first winky face; everyone is plugged in, and it's no longer something to be ashamed of. In fact, one in five relationships begin on an online dating site. Dating on the Web isn't something singles do when they're desperate or lonely; online dating is as legit as meeting originally offline. If you haven't joined, it's time for me to help you sign up and meet The One (or *any*one, depending on your dating preferences).

But regardless of your level of digital dating expertise, this book will transform the Internet into your very own customized dating-empowerment tool. From writing your profile and composing messages to matches to transitioning offline for a date and signing off when you're in a committed relationship, I'll walk you through everything you need to know about flirting in the interwebs.

Shifting to the digital dating world does take a little getting used to, but without a beginning, there would be no end. After all, "happily ever after" doesn't happen without a "once upon a time."

Think of it this way: even though it's called "online dating," it's actually online *meeting* and *offline* dating. While initial developments happen online, lasting relationships happen in person. Putting your profile online *and* taking it down when you meet your perfect match are both iconic moments in life, just like the first time you utter the words "I love you." And that's what I'm here to help you achieve.

But before we get into the nitty-gritty, I need to fill you in on the basics before you log in to the nearest site and commit a digital dating sin. Even if you're an online dating vet, it's likely you picked up a bad habit or two along the way. Hit the Refresh button on your love life by repeating the following vows after me:

The eFlirt Virgin Vows

Putting up a profile is not enough.
You can't simply *be* on an online dating site; you need to *use* it. That means uploading a profile to start but then continuing on by searching for matches, messaging them, responding to standouts in your inbox, and meeting the usernames in person. Acting complacent on a site will yield the same results as acting complacent in life: more nights in your pajamas with Chinese takeout and the company of your cat.

I will not get discouraged by the riffraff.
Usually, any member of a site can message you. That's just a fact. The Delete button is another fact. If someone messages you whom you'd rather not chat with, get rid of him or her

immediately, and move on. Don't let it get you down. It's inevitable that the good, the bad, (and the ugly) will try to chat you up when you're awesome. And nearly every online dating user has received a lewd comment or two in his or her inbox. Negativity from other members means nothing more than the absence of their mother's manners.

It's impossible to message or date one person at a time.
Messaging one match and then praying for him or her to respond is not the most proactive approach. At that rate, you'll be dating online for years, because you never know when or if someone will write back. But once you send multiple messages, be prepared for multiple dates. Don't worry; it's not assumed that you're exclusive until you either spend a significant amount of time together or discuss taking your profiles down.

I won't get emotionally involved until we meet beyond the broadband.
Getting wrapped up in an email string before meeting will earn you a case of the maybes. You know you have the maybes when you start fantasizing about what *could* be rather than what actually *is*. Reserve excitement for when you're face-to-face with your dates so you're positive that your reality matches theirs. Staying in the moment on- and offline will keep your emotions in check.

Freaking out if I don't receive a response is not an option.
Just because your Droid is surgically implanted in the palm of your hand does not mean that the recipient of your message operates the same way. Depending on how often your match logs in, it could be several days before a response makes its way

into your inbox. And sometimes a reply will never come—that's normal. Men typically have lower response rates than women, meaning that they have to write more messages to get one email back. But either way, no online dater will ever have a 100-percent response rate to messages sent . . . unless he or she has sent only a few, of course! Whatever the case, don't take it personally. There are so many reasons matches don't write back: they might not be active on the site anymore, they may be dating someone now but are still checking email, or they could have a busy dating calendar. Dwelling on the silence will only frustrate you.

Gender roles shift on the Web.

It's been said that men should be the aggressors in the dating world. But online dating is an empowerment tool; it's the one time when you don't have to worry about who is approaching whom. After all, you want technology to work *for* you, not against you. While it's great that so many singles are available in one place, you can also get lost in the crowded digital space if you don't remain active. So don't worry about breaking gender "rules"; more traditional roles will develop once you meet in person. While there are a few areas in this book where I give separate tips for ladies and gents, the majority of this advice is meant for both sexes. After all, both should be approaching online dating with similar standards, practices, and outlooks. So while the use of technology does vary for age, gender, and sexual orientation, the advice in this book was particularly written to translate for all.

I will ignore people I know.

If someone you know in your offline life comes across your digital radar, don't send a message unless you're interested in dating him or her. Letting this person have space to flirt sans self-consciousness is more polite than saying hi. Let's face it, you wouldn't want to worry that a coworker is analyzing your profile, either.

Talking on the phone before meeting offline isn't necessary.
Once you're ready to meet up with a match, some prefer to talk on the phone first to get to know each other voice-to-voice, while others skip straight to a date. Singles in less populated areas typically prefer a phone call, but if you're an urbanite, definitely skip dialing your date and meet right away. The only way to truly determine if someone is worth being in the running for your heart is to meet face-to-face.

The guy doesn't always do the asking.
Chivalry exists, but the dynamic is different online. It's still preferred that men ask women out on dates, but not all are in the know on *how* to go about asking digitally. Therefore, it's completely acceptable for a woman to hint that it's time to meet up—or to ask him herself. Remember, you're still developing your dynamic together, and once you meet in person, the gender roles will take their natural course.

Some people play Pinocchio.
It's unfortunate, but some people flub their profiles.

> eFlirt Byte: According to OkCupid, people most often fib about their height by two inches and exaggerate income by 20 percent.

Because the inaccuracies are typically small, it's nothing to be too concerned with but certainly something to be aware of.

I will never give out my last name or personal information.

Even though you've emailed with someone, there's still an element of stranger danger. Giving your full name or other identifying information before meeting allows your date to Google you prior to your first date. Stay in control of your first impression. Ultimately, trust should develop over time, just as with any relationship. Get acquainted on your own terms, not Google's.

I will always meet matches in a public place.

Since you've never met before, meeting in a public place is not only the safest option but also the most comfortable. Being alone together too soon would feel awkward and forced.

I will live and die by spellcheck.

Spelling errors are the cardinal sin of the online world, particularly when dating. It sounds nitpicky, but what would you think if you got an email with a bunch of spelling mistakes in it, particularly if it was a first email and only a few sentences at that? Going the extra mile to proofread will ensure that your correspondence is always pulled together and will be more likely to get a response. There's an easy way to make sure this never happens: download a browser that automatically does the work for you.

It only takes *one*!

With masses of potential partners at your fingertips, your inbox will see more action in a short period of time than you typically do during one evening out. But remember that dating takes patience. If you're in it for love, it only takes one, *The One* who will make your heart skip a byte.

It's about as likely that you'll marry your first kiss as it is that you'll marry the first profile you view. But by the end of this book, you'll know all of the ins and outs of how to make online dating work for *you*—from the photos that will get the most clicks to sexting netiquette. Handy lists are sprinkled throughout so you can return to advice easily during eDating emergencies. And the Internet dating fail and fab moments that the Certified eFlirters and I witness daily (and in bulk) will give you a glimpse into the true life of an online dating coach. (Names and some details are changed to protect the hopeful.)

Fumbling through flirting with your fingertips stops now. Let your journey to eFlirting freedom begin!

Snapshot Skills

PUTTING YOUR BEST FACE FORWARD

When new matches click on your online dating profile, photos are the very first thing they'll see. When you meet online, it's impossible to gauge whether you'll have that *je ne sais quoi* with each other, but photos help determine potential. So don't give your matches a reason to pass you over. Follow these simple tips for uploading fantastic shots that will get you noticed and inspire your profile visitors to click the "email you" button stat.

Your photos are your digital wingman—they talk you up and can get someone interested in meeting you. Just as you wouldn't want a selfish, unkempt, or unreliable wingman, you shouldn't have unsuitable profile pics. Choose your photos just as carefully as you would your pals.

You don't want to end up in a profile photo rut like my client Sean. His eternal modus operandi was to use the same exact full-length photo (hands on hips and airbrushed so heavily it looked one-dimensional) over and over. He then made multiple copies, tilted his feet in different directions so his stance appeared varied, and added different stock images of a bar, a club, or a restaurant for the backdrop of each one so he'd be "virtually" in different locations. But trust me, the ladies were not fooled. And it's not just because his knees don't line up with his ankles—how many twenty-somethings take photos in front of a sweeping staircase . . . in the same suit they wore beachside?

I've seen firsthand how much photo selection matters. Another client, Stella, a longtime online dater in her forties, still hadn't met her match. Although she's a VP on Wall Street, her inbox was flooded with bikers, boozers, and ballers. I knew she was trying to give sexy digital vibes, but her sultry photos were attracting the wrong kinds of men. After I deleted her selects, searched through her photo collection, and uploaded pictures that represented her independent and sassy lifestyle, her entire online dating experience changed for the better.

But don't just take it from me—studies prove that even just having a profile pic in the first place makes you immediately more desirable.

> eFlirt Byte: According to Match.com,
> you're sixteen times more likely to get a
> response with photos than without.

So this is no time to complain that you're not photogenic; it's time to face your recent pictures, pixel by pixel. But before you upload anything, let's delete the photos that should never make their way into digital flirting territory.

Photo Fails

> **Group shots.** Having friends in your photos is never a good idea. If your pal is the same sex as your match, viewers could

conclude that he or she is an ex and that you're not over your old flame or that you date around a lot. On the flip side, if your best shot is with a same-sex friend, your match could get the hots for him or her instead of you. And if there are more than a few pals in the photo, not only do the above issues apply, but it can also be challenging to decipher who you are.

〉 Family photos. If you have children, there's no doubt you have a lot of pictures with them. But including young ones in your profile shows your matches that you're not concerned about your children's privacy, even before they're old enough to join Facebook. Likewise, steer clear of photos with aunts, uncles, Mom, and Dad. Trust me, your online dating profile is not the place for meeting parents; it sets an intimacy level that you haven't yet achieved.

〉 Too much skin. Bikinis and boxers beware! Virtually baring it all isn't just eFlirting, it's the equivalent of a drunken make-out in the dark corner of a bar. If you're looking for a serious relationship, nearly naked photos and sultry stares send the entirely opposite message. So keep your clothes on, and remember that digital sex appeal is all about subtlety—showing a little leg or cleavage can never hurt.

〉 Sans you. Speaking of which, any photos that do not include yourself—like sunsets, pets, and cars—should be avoided. Unless you're a photographer by trade, these photos don't add anything. They just detract from the main event: you!

〉 Black, white, and sepia. Anything less than a full-color photo makes it hard for others to determine your true look and, therefore, chemistry potential. While mobile photo apps and filters such as Instagram are popular, use them sparingly. Something simple like light color saturation is OK, but a washed-out image has the same effect as black-and-white.

〉 **Disguises.** Hats, sunglasses, and anything else that covers your face should be avoided. You want to evoke confidence, and hiding behind these things has the opposite effect. If you must upload a photo inspired by celebrity camouflage, stick to one, and make sure that you balance it with others where you can clearly see your whole face.

〉 **Self-portraits.** Photos taken by yourself, whether in the mirror, at arm's length, or on a webcam should be deleted ASAP. These photos never capture your best angle. And let's face it, the poor-man's-photographer approach points out that either your social life is lacking or you're embarrassed to ask a friend to snap a shot of you.

So Ctrl + Alt + Delete all photos that fit these criteria from your dating life.

Picture Perfect

Now, to put your best face forward, follow my rules for profile photo perfection.

〉 **Two to three close-ups.** Without the ability to see your face clearly, your match will have a tough time determining if he or she finds you attractive. Upload a few close-ups, and make one your main pic. You want to strike an approachable attitude, from facial expression to body language, so showing your pearly whites in at least one of these images is a must. Avoid any telltale standoffish signs like crossed arms or scowls.

> eFlirt Byte: OkCupid's study on profile pictures reveals that women get the most messages when they're making a flirty face in their main photo, while men get the best results if they're looking slightly off-camera.

However, keep in mind that OkCupid's demographics tend to skew a bit younger than, say, eHarmony. Blowing a kiss to the camera might work on OkCupid, but a simple smile will work best on less quirky sites.

❭ One to two action shots. Providing your match with a sense of your lifestyle gives instant authenticity to your profile. Upload a photo of you skiing, singing, snorkeling, or doing whatever interests you most. It's OK if you're not entirely distinguishable in this shot, since you'll have other clear images in your profile—as long as you don't look unattractive. As a bonus, action photos are great conversation starters. If you're swishing down the Alps and your match also loves skiing, you've given him or her an easy way to connect with you. Questions inspired by your photos are inevitable, so make sure you're doing something conversation-worthy; think guitar strumming instead of chowing down. Without a good story to back up the photo, your emails to each other could fall flat.

❭ One to two full-length pictures. Showing off your bod in a modest way will help you snag your perfect partner. There's no need to hide; eventually, you're going to have an in person date, so your match will get to see your goods in complete Technicolor glory. Flaunt what you've got with flattering, form-fitting clothes. Full-length photos also give your match the opportunity to check out your personal style from head to toe.

> **Represent the real-time you.** While your online dating profile might not be a living, breathing Web page like your Facebook Timeline, it's still important to represent who you are and what you look like today. So if you color your hair, grow a goatee, or cut your locks, your photos need to correspond. If your look is a revolving door, make sure that different photos represent a variety of the person your match might meet. If you wear contacts and glasses, post photos of both. Likewise, you want to represent your age, weight, and body shape accurately. Own those ten pounds you recently put on or the five you lost. Uploading photos from that one time seven years ago when you trained for a triathlon and were at the peak of physical shape won't attract someone who will love you for the real-time you. Even if you think you look the same today as you did a few years ago, avoid uploading photos that are more than two years old so your match has the latest—and greatest—first impression. Remember, the real-time you will attract a real-time match.

> **Cropping makes you clickable.** Don't take any of these must-have photos at face value. Whether you're cutting out food from a table or an ex's hand that is entwined with yours, removing unnecessary distractions is always a good thing. Editing can even enhance photos that were taken professionally. For example, cropping a photo closely to one side of your face will remove symmetry to give the image a more casual look.

eFlirt Byte: HowAboutWe finds that users who upload at least three photos get twice as many messages as those with only one shot.

Ideally, you want to upload five to seven photos to give your match a complete picture of who you are. But if you don't have all of these in your arsenal, three will do for now.

And of course, if you have some favorite shots of yourself above and beyond this list of must-haves, feel free to upload an extra image or two. You are your own best judge. Just be sure not to go overboard—using more than ten photos is overwhelming.

When I met my client Chris, he had nineteen photos uploaded to Match.com. Even though he was the kind of guy women would swoon over in person—handsome, educated, successful, and adventurous—his inbox was empty. I deleted all but six, and his inbox quickly filled up. You want matches to view your photos quickly, move on to reading your profile, and then message you. If it takes too long to complete one of these steps, you could lose them along the way.

The order of your pictures matters, too. The most important are your main pic and the last image—the initial and final impressions. So start with a close-up as your main photo, and end with your favorite from the rest of the bunch. In the middle, mix in your personality. Ideally, no two photos from the same categories should be side-by-side so you give the appearance of living a full lifestyle. The best order might be something like (1) close-up, (2) full-length, (3) close-up, (4) action shot, (5) full-length, (6) close-up, (7) action shot. Once they're up, there's no need to rotate the order much. Your main picture is the one you'll want to update about every two months to keep things fresh, so either swap it out for another great close-up that's already live on your page or upload a new one to give your profile a new look.

You probably already have photos that fit the profile photo must-have categories. But if you don't, it's time to start snapping some new shots. Uploading the best of your archives will do for now, though; it's most important to move your dating life forward.

In the meantime, new photos can be taken by pals, or you can hire a professional photographer. Everyone has a different comfort level for lookin' good. But regardless of how you're going about snapping new shots, the real secret to amazing up-to-date shots is in the primping and the prep.

Primping

Wardrobe is crucial. Clothes are the Web 2.0 equivalent of non-verbal communication. So keep these outfit tips in mind:

VARIETY

When you're snapping new photos, it's important to switch up your outfits. Keep to my strict one-photo-per-outfit rule. No matter how fabulous you look in that black tank, three photos in one shirt will strike only one virtual note. Wearing the same outfit more than once not only means that your matches get to see just one side of who you are, but in the worst-case scenario, they might skip over your profile because that look doesn't resonate with them. Glam it up for a shot of you in a little black dress (ladies) or a jacket (gents), dress it down with jeans and a tee, and get sporty if you're active. Mixing and matching different looks from your life—from casual to semiformal—give your match multiple opportunities to find you attractive.

COLOR

For a woman, red is the best color you can wear in your main photo. Not only will it instantly jump out from the otherwise drab montage of black, gray, brown, and white outfits in your matches' search results, but it's also been scientifically proven that "red" is for "relationship."

> **eFlirt Byte:** A study at the University of Rochester examined the responses of men viewing pictures of women in different-colored outfits. In every single instance, the photos of women wearing red were rated significantly more attractive or sexually desirable.

For men, the masses tend to stick to earth tones, which means you should avoid them at all costs. Skip white, gray, black, and tan. These colors can make you blend into the background of a Web page, particularly when you're being viewed in a small thumbnail. Go bold, but make sure the color you pick flatters your skin tone. If you tan well and have pink undertones to your skin, stick to cool shades like purple, blue, and pink. If you burn often in the sun and have yellow undertones, don warm hues like green, yellow, orange, and red. And if you're not sure which of these makes the most sense but you have brilliant green or blue eyes, matching your clothes to your eye color will always make your skin glow.

Regardless of gender, solid colors always look best on-camera, so skip small, tight patterns. If you're going to go with a print, make it bold so it's clear what's going on in the image.

KEEP IT SIMPLE

Don't go too over-the-top with your wardrobe styling. One of my sixty-five-year-old clients posted a glamour shot of herself in a studded bra as her main photo! Her other favorite profile photos included a sheer dress sans bra, a full-on salsa-dancing outfit, and a skirt suit with a dramatic wide-brimmed, 1940s-style hat. Showing pixel personality is important, but the purpose of taking photos is to focus on capturing the essence of who you are in your everyday life.

Prepping

Even with the most amazing outfits, your shoot can fall apart if you fail at the prep work. Tick off each item below to ensure that you're ready to get in front of the lens.

❯ **Ask questions now.** If you have any hesitations, don't wait until the day of your shoot to talk to whoever is taking your pics. Having peace of mind will help calm your nerves. See the "Going Pro" section below for the types of questions you might want to ask.

❯ **Don't pregame.** Drinking too much—the night before or during the shoot—will read in photos. Admit it, hungover or tipsy is never your best look.

❯ **Pack wisely.** Bring hair product, makeup, deodorant, and any other primping items to refresh yourself throughout the shoot. When in doubt, throw it in your bag.

❭ Be on time. Respect other people's time by showing up a few minutes early. In the most extreme case, running late—particularly for a professional photographer—might mean a shorter shoot and not getting all of the right photos for your profile.

❭ Sleep. A full night's rest is worth its weight in gold. Feel guilt-free about going to bed early the night before so you're fresh-faced for the shoot.

❭ Pay up front. If you're compensating the person behind the lens for his or her time, take care of payment in advance. Even if the photographer doesn't ask you to pay ahead of time, it's best to get this out of the way so you can be completely focused on the task at hand, instead of wondering where the closest ATM is.

❭ Relax. Laugh at yourself for doing this—it's OK! Taking a light-hearted approach to the whole situation will calm your demeanor and body language, allowing the best shots to come through the lens.

Going Pro

A trend I've noticed from working with hundreds of singles is that older and younger generations have opposite reactions to professional photos. Of course, this doesn't apply to every-one but typically, twenty-somethings think professional photos are a little lame and reveal a lack of social life. Meanwhile, the fifty-plus crowd find professional shots a turn-on because they indicate that their match is successful enough to hire a photographer.

Regardless of your age, sometimes you just want to bring in a professional photographer to get the right shots. The important lesson is that younger singles should direct the photographer to take not-so-polished, lifestyle-type snapshots, images that don't look so pro. More mature singles should get some relaxed shots, too, but focus at least half of the shoot on more professional-looking headshots. Either way, make sure you choose a photographer who has experience taking photos specifically for dating profiles. And ask to see examples of his or her work prior to booking. Head to the Resource section at eFlirtExpert.com/loveatfirstclick for recommendations in your area.

Since the goal is to make the pictures appear as natural as possible, a studio with one backdrop is not ideal. Outdoor shoots offer the most variety, but being indoors can work if the space is multidimensional. Ask in advance if the studio offers different settings, like a couch, a stairwell, or a window. Avoid obvious poses so your body language appears as natural as possible (no hand-on-cheek action!), and ask your photographer to frame shots so they're not all perfectly composed. To get the most bang for your buck, make sure your shoot allows for at least three wardrobe changes.

Remember that the lighting of a professional studio is different from your bathroom vanity, so makeup—even for men—will help your complexion look more true to life in the final shot when you consider the harsh bulbs. If you're clueless when it comes to makeup, it's best to hire someone in the know. If you're already going pro with a photographer, it makes sense to invest in a professional makeup artist, too. But if that's not in your budget, I got the skinny from Stefanie Syat, a high-fashion makeup artist in NYC and the founder of Pre-Dame Makeup Party, a service for ladies that glams you up before going out. But don't worry, guys, she's worked on plenty of male mugs during her photo-shoot experience, too. Here are her tips for getting picture-perfect.

Makeup Must-Haves

› **Ladies.** Use a sheer foundation that evens out your skin tone, but don't cake it on. Focus around your nose to reduce redness. Powdering your T-zone is a must for indoor shoots—the artificial light picks up more textures than natural light. Avoid shimmer, too. Lighting can make a sparkly area appear oily instead of effervescent, so use matte eye shadows, and try to find a bronzer without shimmer. As long as they don't leave you sparkly, bronzers do a great job of warming up your skin tone for the camera. Curl eyelashes, apply two coats of mascara on top and bottom, let it dry, and then curl them again. Special attention to lashes will make your eyes appear larger on-camera. If you're shooting outside, apply your makeup as usual, but make sure to pack an extra pop of color on those cheeks—the sun tends to wash them out.

› **Men.** Ask a female friend to dab some concealer on just the spots. If your skin has more trouble than just a few blemishes, buy a foundation that is yellow-based. Men tend to have more redness and uneven skin tones, so the yellow will help diminish that. Aim for a sheer finish product—a novice application of full coverage can look cakey. But a little powder for your forehead and near the hairline is a must to reduce shine.

For hair, just make sure it looks the way it normally does. If your locks are usually straight, don't curl them. Your photos should look just like the you that your matches will meet. But if you wear your hair curly one day and straight the next, upload photos with both looks.

After the photo shoot, digital retouching should only be an option for daters with wrinkles and age spots that appear more pronounced under lighting, and even then, photos should be edited as minimally as possible. In general, airbrushing and other digital techniques will remove the authenticity of the photos and turn off potential matches.

But face it, you're not always glossed up! So after your shoot, mix the pro's shots with a few from your own photo albums.

Digital DIY

If you'd rather use a pal as your photographer, here are seven things to remember before the camera starts clicking.

1. Environment. Vary locations as often as your outfits. Diversity will speak to your lifestyle, whether you're at home cooking, lounging at your local coffee shop, or dressed up for an event. You're ultimately aiming to capture a day in the life of you.

2. Lighting. A well-lit environment is crucial so your photos don't appear grainy. Low-resolution snapshots can look old, and you don't want your match to question whether the picture was taken recently.

3. Props. Friends who aren't natural-born photographers will find that getting the perfect shot is easiest when more props are involved. Activities encourage those caught-in-motion shots, so create your signature omelet, grab a mug of something steamy, or pick up a tennis racket. Using a prop will make you look natural in the snapshot.

4. Expression. Experiment with different angles and facial expressions. Smile, laugh, and try simply to relax your face. More options offer a greater chance of capturing that perfect pose.

5. Stance. According to Gordon Gooch, founder of Dating Headshots.com, a nationwide network of professional photographers who specialize in profile photos, sometimes you have to exaggerate your body stance in particular ways to get the best shots. Never face the camera head-on, as this will make you appear wider. He advises focusing on three things: shoulders, posture, and arms. Start by turning sideways to the camera and putting your weight on your back leg. Next, point your front toes toward the camera with a slight bend in the front knee. Then rotate your front shoulder away from the camera. If you suck in your stomach, you'll be forced to stand taller. For posture, extend your chin toward the camera, and simultaneously push your shoulders back. This will nicely distinguish your head from your body. If you're sitting, inch your way to the edge of the chair while still presenting more of one side to the camera, and rotate your front shoulder back. As for your arms and hands, never leave them hanging by your side—that will make you look wider. Try moving your elbows slightly away from your body so that the camera sees light between your elbow and your body, and then put at least one hand in your pocket.

6. Framing. Keep in mind that without a professional on hand, you'll need to be your own art director. Recommend that your friend frame photos in a mixture of compositions: from the shoulders up, from the waist up, and even a few wide photos to capture more background.

7. No critics allowed. As the "talent" for the day, you are not allowed to look through the viewfinder. You'll want to—and most people do, in social settings—but don't! Critiquing photos too early can seriously hinder your results. When I did a casual shoot with my client Brynn to balance out her professional headshots with more relaxed shots, she kept pulling the camera out of my hands to sneak a peek. Throughout the day, she became more and more introverted, and when you become inhibited, the shoot won't produce the relaxed photos you need for your profile.

I know this can all be overwhelming, but the main thing to keep in mind is not to stress if it takes you a week or two to shoot, gather, crop, and post the right photos to your profile. It's worth the time and effort, because having the right pictures online brings you one step closer to love offline. Photos offer up the first impression, and if they're done right, it won't be the last.

CHAPTER 2

Wink Wide Web

CHOOSING THE RIGHT DATING SITE

The most common question I get asked is, "What's the best online dating site?" But the truth is that there isn't a *best*.

If there were indeed a universal unrivaled site, there would be only one. But instead, there are thousands of sites and apps, increasing by the month. Enter the age of the Wink Wide Web.

Every site is good for someone, but no site is good for everyone. You can meet *someone* no matter what site you join . . . but that doesn't mean he or she will be your right click. My client Trey was on Match.com and not meeting many ladies he liked. So I recommended that he try OkCupid, where I thought he'd have more cyber-luck. One ghostwritten profile, a few months, and a bunch of emails later, he received a ping from a beauty. "I've never written to a guy before, but your profile was so compelling that I just had to say HI!" When they met up, drinks turned into dinner, which turned into talking all night. And now they're married!

Had Trey stayed on his original dating site, they would

have never met. Different sites are often made up of completely different communities. Switching can mean the difference between visiting Los Angeles and Birmingham. Each site's crowd has trends of members with distinct personalities, interests, backgrounds, and dating goals. Too often, singles try a site, have an unfulfilling experience, and swear off online dating altogether. But it could simply be that the site you're on just isn't the right fit.

That's the most challenging part of a fragmented online dating space: you could be on one site while your ideal match browses another. The key to ensuring that your match is only a mouse click away is confidence in what you're searching for.

Who, Who, Who To Woo

Your best aid in ensuring that you meet your right click is knowing yourself and having a clear idea of what your match might resemble. We'll focus a lot on *you* in chapter 3, but first, let's focus on what you want in your mate.

YOUR DREAM DATE

1. Put it all down. We all have a list of criteria for what we're looking for in a match. Whether it's a mental note in the back of your mind or written in a spiral-bound notebook hidden under your mattress, you know you have the likes and dislikes of your next love stashed away somewhere. So what are you looking for in a match? If you haven't already written this down, it's time to put pen to paper. Keep this private; sharing means judgment and editing. This exercise should be a safe space for you to uncover your desires. It will also clarify your intention: are you looking for love, a fling, or something in between? Let your list be your guide.

2. Mate traits. Now that you've put it all out there, it's time to prioritize. Choose your three most important qualities in a match, and focus on them as you move forward. Remove relationship essentials that any good match should have because they're qualities of a successful partnership, like "honesty" and "trustworthiness." Instead, focus on attributes that would specifically appeal to you, such as "thrill seeker" or "laid-back."

3. Define your boundaries. Knowing your deal breakers is also important. Nearly everyone I meet has a few absolute conditions. For example, a marathon runner who values health said he could never date a smoker. Depending on your criteria, you can often filter your dating site searches so that matches who fall within a certain category don't cross your computer screen. This will allow you to be a more efficient online dater. Just be sure not to limit yourself too much; deal breakers are absolute conditions that you could never fit into your lifestyle, not things you'd just prefer to live without.

4. Remain open-minded. No one's perfect, so know that your match will differ from your expectations. But this does not mean you're settling; in the best cases, your matches will exceed everything you thought you wanted. Online dating allows you the opportunity to search outside the inbox and see what else exists. Don't feel that you're confined by your list—it's simply a jumping-off point so you know what to avoid and what's most important to you.

My client Mala's experience is the perfect example of how online dating is an opportunity to date beyond your usual type. She was a partner at a prestigious law firm, well traveled, and yet still silly. But although she had a luxurious lifestyle, her taste in men was less than refined. Ms. Penthouse wanted a tatted-up, Harley-riding macho man. I know better than anyone that "the heart wants what the heart wants," but trust me, hers did not want *this*. Mala's past relationship experience with said type was more horrific than *The Texas Chainsaw Massacre,* and it was obvious that this kind of guy just wasn't working out for her.

With her online dating passwords in hand, I showcased Mala's endearing qualities to the men of Chemistry.com through her profile, looked for her soul mate on her behalf, and engaged gentlemen in banter as intriguing as she is in real life. I knew I'd find her a guy who was as high-caliber as her Christian Louboutin stilettos.

But she didn't want any of the men I sent to her. She got emotional. She was stubborn. And she started to despise me. Soon it didn't matter if the guy had everything she asked for— she was always negative. I finally managed to persuade her to accept a date with someone she was less than enthused about. And she totally fell for him. Mala learned my number one lesson for online daters the hard way: it's unlikely that you're going to love your match on paper.

In fact, you probably won't! To be date-worthy, someone simply needs to intrigue you and make you want to know more. If the person seems worth a margarita, go out together. Being too discerning before you meet could mean inadvertently passing over your next relationship. Especially when you're new to online dating and not used to viewing your matches side-by-side on a computer screen (which will inevitably make you quick to judge one against another), if you view a profile and think "maybe," say "yes."

Site Strategy

There are two main categories of dating sites: those that give you independence and those that play matchmaker. Neither is better; they're just different user experiences. You might find that you prefer one approach to another, so here are the specifics.

On *search-based sites,* you're in control of your eDestiny. You can search as far and wide as you desire. You can check out different types of people, age ranges, and heights, changing your preferences with your every whim. The interweb is your oyster—you can even search other zip codes. To some singles, like my client Jared, this is an integral part of their strategy. He lived in Tacoma but traveled to San Francisco for half of every workweek. When your life is split between two cities, it can be challenging to meet someone. But with online dating, he was able to set up dates in both cities to increase his chances.

For Jared—and for all search-based eDaters—being proactive about finding a mate and making sure you're in the best position to meet him or her is how you'll get the most out of your experience.

On *algorithm-centric sites,* a select number of matches is delivered to you daily, typically with a maximum amount of allotted selections. You'll truly get your money's worth by checking in every day, which requires dedication. Many sites of this nature won't send more matches until you clear out your queue, so frequent log-ins to review potentials will get the best results.

I'll teach you how to optimize your experiences on both kinds of sites in chapter 7. But while functionality might define the approach you take to dating, it's not the most important part of deciding which site to join.

A dating site is only as good as your matches on it.
When I met George, a thirty-seven-year-old New Yorker, he was already two ex-wives in the hole. With the sex drive of an eighteen-year-old, the maturity of a college student, and the wallet most forty-year-olds crave, he was the ultimate bachelor. But after years of focusing on beauty over brains, he was ready for an intellectual connection. He promised me that he wanted to change, begged me to work with him, and professed his undying desire for his first truly meaningful relationship.

But at the time, he was a member of the "elite sugar daddy dating site," SeekingArrangement.com. It doesn't take an eFlirt Expert to realize that it was unlikely that he'd meet The One on a site where the ladies required private jets to Rio each weekend. Ditching SeekingArrangement and opting in to Match.com committed George to his new intentions.

There's more to selecting a site than choosing the one with the cutest couple in its TV commercial. Regardless of how much fun a site is to use or how polished the design, the value is in the matches you'll meet.

Don't judge a site by its cover . . . or its cover charge. Free sites often get a bad rap, but in today's techie world, many are no less reputable than paid ones. Most singles assume that the matches on sites sans charge are not worth as much from a dating perspective. But whether they think the people on free sites are cyber–Peeping Toms or booty beggars, it's simply not true. I've seen nearly as many lasting love connections happen via freebies as I have on paid sites. What defines a site—free or paid—is its community. So price shouldn't matter unless it's a budgetary concern. The most important part of online dating is whether your matches make your heart go pitter-patter.

When zero dollars are required to subscribe, there are still some possibilities to prep yourself for:

Casual members. Nearly every dating site has users with varying levels of seriousness. But in general, free sites do have a higher number of casual members. Keeping an eye out for red flags in your matches' profiles is more relevant on sites with lower barriers to email. (See chapter 8 for these red flags.)

Delete, delete. You can expect to get more messages that inspire you to hit the Delete key. Of course, receiving messages from matches who don't inspire a reply will happen on every site. Anyone who's a member of a site—or who gets matched with you, if you're on an algorithm-based site—can drop you an email. But on free sites, you can expect more messages from matches outside your ideal target, because it's easier for people to put up a profile on a whim and message en masse without much thought.

Paused profiles. On any site, you might come across users who stop logging in for long stretches. But inactive users are even more common on free sites, because users often join non-committally but don't follow through with the process. Be on the lookout for inactive profiles, and make checking their last log-ins a habit before reaching out.

Let's address the particulars of site selection, regardless of cost. Here are the things you should consider before making yourself a permanent part of a site's community.

All Systems Go

PLAY BEFORE YOU PAY

Before you exchange your credit-card digits for a membership, join for free and take a peek at your local matches. Most sites allow you to do this. You won't be able to contact anyone without purchasing, but this way you'll be able to scope out potential partners before you officially join a community. If your matches don't fit your preferences—body, mind, or profile—delete your account and try out a new site. Membership discounts and free trials can be found on the Resources page at eFlirtExpert.com /loveatfirstclick.

For sites that deliver matches to you via algorithm, you can also usually first join and view your matches for free. After a week or so, decide if there are enough clickable mates to sign up for a full-access membership.

PUT YOUR MONEY WHERE YOUR MOUTH IS

When you're pondering different subscription options on paid sites, think long-term. If you've done your homework and found several pages of matches that strike your fancy, sign up for at least three months. Note that it will likely take you a bit of time to adjust when taking your love life digital. Committing to more than one month will give you time to work through the kinks and help you resist the temptation to flee simply because you're outside your comfort zone.

There's also typically a cost savings when joining for a predetermined amount of time rather than going month-to-month. In fact, some sites like Match.com will give you a "guarantee." If you choose the six-month option and don't find a match within that time frame, you'll get six more months free. While a complimentary membership may be alluring, be sure to read the fine print before committing. There are often restrictions on the amount of activity that is required during your first six months.

But if your site du jour has only a small community of singles in your area or you see less than a few solid pages of potentials, subscribe for one month so you can get the full experience first before making an informed decision about the long term. Regardless, know that most sites will auto-renew your membership if you don't cancel, so be sure to set a calendar reminder for a few days before your subscription is up to assess whether you want to let the renewal go through, change your monthly commitment, or cancel completely.

THE TWO-SITE RULE

You should always have active profiles on at least two sites. This will allow you to access a wider variety of clickable matches (and be available to more potentials, too). Being in two communities means that your profile is constantly in front of the right people.

It's best to join one big site and one niche site. If you're new to online dating or have limited time, this will alleviate match overload, since niche sites are typically smaller communities than large mainstream sites. If you're on a budget, join one free site and one paid community to stretch your dollars and sense. Once you're a vet, you'll be able to manage more than two at a time, but don't exceed active accounts on more than four at once. If you're not seeing much traction on a site, it's better to hide your profile and return later so you get new-member status.

As soon as my client Jimmy signed his divorce papers, he joined every site a search engine could find. From SingleParent Meet to eHarmony and MillionaireMatch to ChristianMingle, his Gmail was overflowing with notifications from fifteen sites! While the potential for meeting so many people was exciting to him, he was quickly overwhelmed and got partner-potential paralysis. Sometimes too many options can lead to a defocused dating life. Keeping things to three sites at a time means your date calendar is full, but not overwhelmed.

HOT-SPOT HOPPING

When there aren't many matches for you to reach out to on a site, you'll maximize your time, energy and moolah by jumping to a new community. Leave that site behind, and if you're still single and mingling a few months later, come back and review its new members. Just don't jump ship until you've stayed at least a month so you know you've had a full experience on that site and didn't overlook any clickable matches.

Changing sites from time to time—and then revisiting—is the best strategy, especially for the forty-plus crowd. As you age, the quantity of available singles naturally decreases, but that doesn't mean that *quality* mates aren't available. To find them, you need to be proactive about site hopping. Remember, it only takes One!

NICHE VALUE

Bigger isn't always better. Whether it's a particular religion, hobby, or ethnicity, niche sites have a few unique strengths that you should tap into. It goes without saying that they'll give you more targeted match potential, since you'll have an immediate commonality with the other online daters. And niche sites also often attract singles who might otherwise skip online dating.

eFlirt Byte: According to Sparkology.com,
a luxury dating site for young professionals,
31 percent of its users are first time
online daters.

The added value of niche sites is that you might not otherwise virtually run into some of their members. It's also common for smaller communities to have more engaged users, which more easily results in offline dates.

eFlirt Byte: On Tastebuds.fm, a site
that matches singles by their
music preferences, 43 percent of first
messages from users receive a reply
(compared with 32 percent on OkCupid).

Every site is its own experience, unique to each eDater.
No, this is not a disclaimer at the bottom of the TV screen—it's the truth. You and your BFF could have completely different luck on the same exact site. Unless you're the same age and living in the same city, with similar personalities, seeking the twin of your ideal match, the same sites will likely suit each of you differently. And that's something to be aware of as you browse for your right click (and inevitably dish to your friends about it along the way). Others' opinions shouldn't sway you, and vice versa, because everyone's experience is unique.

While a site has a general community, things vary based on location. In one state or city, a site might be more focused on hookups for twenty-somethings, with only a few singles in their fifties. But in a different locale, it could be boomer-relationship heaven.

To help singles navigate this confusion and stay on top of newly launched innovations, I've developed eFlirt Engine. It's not a dating site; rather, it finds the best site for you based on your individual wants and needs using my knowledge of sites, user behavior, and eDating trends. It digitizes the process I've used for recommending sites to singles for years. So, if you're unsure of which site to join, use eFlirtEngine.com as a starting point.

But all sites do have target demographics that they strive to attract. It's easier for big sites to achieve this than for the smaller ones, though. The age of their business, quantity of users, and advertising dollars ensure more control over who joins. For mainstream sites, these demographics—and the pros and cons—are universally true, regardless of age, city, or personality. So let's speed date each of the big online dating sites (see table 1).

Table 1. Pros and Cons of Mainstream Sites

SITE	PRO	CON
Chemistry.com	Chemistry selects daily matches for you, ideal for singles who are pressed for time. As a bonus, the traffic boom during its free communication weekends is likely to score you a date.	If you want to be the master of your own destiny, you might feel limited, since you can't search far and wide.
eHarmony.com	Created for relationship-minded singles, eHarmony's patented Compatibility Matching System delivers select matches to your inbox. And the proof is in the pudding: the site accounts for 542 marriages a day, which is 5 percent of all nuptials in the United States.	The site's guided communication makes sure that you and a match click before you meet, but this means the communication process itself can take time. Don't always expect a quick date.
HowAboutWe.com	Known as the offline dating site, HowAboutWe lets you meet matches based on interests and activities. You propose dates, like "How about we see a photography exhibit and grab a tea afterward?" It's great for singles on the move who crave new experiences.	If you're wary of getting offline quickly with your match, this might not be the right pick for you, since the focus is moving the conversation off the screen ASAP.

SITE	PRO	CON
JDate.com	If dating a mensch is a must in your life, JDate is the leader in mass-market appeal, responsible for more Jewish marriages than all other dating sites combined. While other sites may have "chosen" members, JDate allows you to search by denomination.	Sometimes non-Jews crash the virtual party, so if you're exclusively looking for a Jewish match, be wary of members who leave the "Religion" field blank.
Match.com	Boasting more than 20 million members, Match is one of the largest online dating communities. Unlike other large sites, you can get incredibly targeted when finding matches. Its search function is one of the best in the biz, allowing you to filter your matches by twenty-six individual criteria.	With such a large community of singles, you might have to invest more time and energy into being proactive than you would on smaller sites.
OkCupid.com	OkCupid is a free site with quirky features that get addictive, feeling almost more like a social network than a dating site. But it's still brainy; they use math to get you dates. Although you have free rein to search, the site shows you the percentage of your match with each eSuitor.	Since it's a free community, you might get more messages than normal from your dating D-listers.

SITE	PRO	CON
PlentyofFish.com	PlentyofFish (POF) is one of the largest dating sites and also boasts free membership. Its approach is casual and simple—no fifteen-question profiles here. Pop some minimal information into the site, and you're good to start flirting.	Since the profile is sparse, that also means you have a limited amount of info on your matches.

In addition to the mainstream sites, there are literally thousands of other sites out there. To help you sort through the options, I've created a Resources page at eFlirtExpert.com/loveatfirst click. New sites launch all the time, and many go in and out of trend quickly. So proceed on to new sites with caution, and make sure you experience them sans membership before you join.

When evaluating a site, focus on the active matches you see and your experience rather than reviews. Everyone's time online is individual, so a site's effectiveness can't be generalized Yelp-style. New technology is fun, but make sure you are always putting your heart first.

CHAPTER 3

Self-Digitize

WRITING THE PERFECT PROFILE

In the Winkisphere, your photos and text make up your profile and are the very first impression to a match. This means that when someone views your profile, it's often your make-or-break moment, the nanosecond when the person decides whether to message you or skip to the next hopeful in his or her queue.

The first dating profile I ever wrote was exactly seven characters long, yet it was wildly successful (keep in mind this was back in 1996): "15/F/MA." For those of you who didn't partake in old-school AOL chat rooms, that was my age, sex, and location (A/S/L), the digital mating call, version 1.0.

Long after my parents were fast asleep, I'd sneak down to the living room, turn on our family's Dell desktop, log in, and pronounce to the cyberverse that I was single and eMingling. Soon enough, I'd be swooning over hotrod8723, who identified himself as 17/M/KS. An older man—be still, my virtual heart!

Although the famous "You've got mail" notification lives on in memory, profiles are now much more complex than just a few mundane characters. Rather than focusing purely on facts such as your age, you're expected to be clever and original. Different sites ask different questions. And some profiles get lengthy—eHarmony users must fill out a 258-question survey before they can make their profile live!

But there's a good reason for this new-school approach. More sophisticated profiles and tools let you connect better with a match before meeting in person. And with so many people meeting online today, you need more search filters just to find the sorts of matches you seek.

Of course, this is a double-edged sword. Given that there are millions of singles online, dating can sometimes feel as competitive as *The Amazing Race*. Quantity rules, which, of course, means that you can easily be passed over for a match with a better tagline. What's a single to do when all of the things that take place in person—smile, intrigue, vibe, and flirt—have to be conveyed on virtual paper?!

eFlirting Begins with Your Username

This is the first piece of text a match will see, so it's important to give it some thought. You don't want to risk someone uttering "whoa" when your username pops up in his or her search results.

This happened to my client Nina, a thirty-something Phoenix gal who was super sweet, into the outdoors, and looking to settle down. But she was giving guys the impression that she had a wild side. When I first saw that her username was MidnightSeductress, I thought it had to be a mistake. But when I plugged it into the dating site letter for letter, there she was. If flings were on her agenda, this would have been fine, but since she was looking for a serious commitment, her username was sending entirely the wrong message.

Don't try to impress based on what you think others want; make sure your username reflects your own personality. Here are a few tips to keep in mind when you're naming your digital self.

> **Combine interests.** Combining hobbies or words on the same topic is an easy way to stand out from the crowd. For example, if you love travel, you might go with something like GlobalTrek or OutdoorVentures.

> **Make up your own word.** It's OK if your username can't be found in Webster's. Taking creativity one step further, you can create a word to represent you, no definition required—for example, Gigglation or Explorcation.

> **Keep your virtual clothes on.** Save the intimate implications for later on; usernames with sexual undertones can send the wrong impression. I know some women who won't even open emails from guys with inappropriate terms or, ahem, "69." For women, usernames like Nina's can imply that you're looking for a more casual connection, where getting nookie on the first night is acceptable.

> **Don't use your birth name.** Real names and nicknames should be nixed from your digital dating details. Consider your real name the virtual equivalent of whispering sweet nothings—it's special and should be reserved for someone you're crushin' on. This info also makes it easy for people to search and identify details of your life before you're ready to reveal them. Your digital footprint is essentially a portal to your past, so protect it until you've met someone in person and made a true first impression.

> The numbers game. Your username is not a numerology report, so stay away from numbers. This will allow you to remain unique rather than pointing out that you're the eighteenth person to choose "citygal." Revealing personal details through numbers is also a no-no. Your birthday reveals your age in the wrong context, your lucky number will be irrelevant to anyone but you, and the current year will quickly become dated, pointing out just how long you've been on the eDating scene. Needless to say, none of this adds to the conversation.

Writing Your Profile

Beyond your screen name and photos, what you choose to say in your profile is the most critical element of virtual attraction. Because of this, it's common to feel as if you want to check out the competition—you know, what's that *other* hottie with a damn good body saying?

Resist the urge to search for your doppelgänger before you write your profile. Getting stuck on someone else's words and style will only make your profile sound like everyone else's. Let's make sure that your profile stands out from the pack, speaks to the person *you* are, and catches the attention of the right eBachelor or eBachelorette.

This is your opportunity to be uniquely you and generate interest in others to meet you. Remember that this isn't a formal business bio, an old-school personal ad, a creative-writing assignment, or an opportunity to peddle your personal website. Avoid talking too much about work, and steer clear of other common pitfalls like listing trite interests ("long walks on the beach"), showing off with poetry, or pasting links to your art portfolio.

To strike the right digital tone, apply a little strategy to your thought process.

MARKETING TO YOUR MATCH

In the marketing world, certain principles are applied to each campaign, and let's face it, putting up a profile is a bit like marketing your singledom. Here are the lessons I learned while marketing for the Fortune 500s that apply here, too.

› Audience. Know what types of matches you're trying to reach with your profile. Revisit your dream-date list from chapter 2 to make sure you're in the know on this one. Understanding your ideal audience will not only allow you to have a more targeted approach, but it will also provide a way to measure cyber-success. Are you receiving emails from the right people? Are your dates as good in person as they were on paper? Are you going on just as many second dates as first dates?

› Key messages. Think about what you're projecting to your wanna-be match. You should be sending at least three underlying vibes. Keep them in mind as you write, and make sure there are themes that are reinforced throughout the text. For example, if you want to convey intelligence, don't use the word directly. Instead, show it through word choice and smarty-pants interests.

› The Power of Three. Romance might call for two to create the perfect couple, but in marketing, three is the power number. Psychological studies say that the mind can easily grasp threes. Throw in a fourth, and things get confusing; keep it to two, and there might not be enough information for someone to process and feel comfortable. This magic number allows you to show diversity, too. So stick to three interests, three words to describe your ideal match, or three favorite movies. (Even that list is a three-parter!)

❯ Call to action. All marketing promotions feature a call to action, something that encourages people to make a purchase, visit a website, or like them via social media. For online dating, direct calls to action, such as "Message me if you want to know more," convey that you lack confidence. But interaction can be encouraged in other, less obvious ways. Creating intrigue by introducing topics and revealing only enough to whet their digital palate will inspire conversation, as will being specific about what interests you. Mentioning your favorite band in your profile, for example, is a subliminal call to action for other fans of the genre or live music.

❯ Conversion through simplicity. It's unlikely that you'll find a Nike ad that contains an entire page of ten-point-font copy. While this was popular during the 1960's (a la *Mad Men*), today you're more likely to feel intimidated and immediately flip the page, begin to read but lose interest halfway through, or simply skim. The same can happen to your online dating profile. The best ads feature a compelling image, brief copy, and a call to action. Similarly, your profile features photos, a description, and a call to action. But what differs is that you're not something your match is familiar with . . . yet. You want to showcase more information than a typical advert, but it shouldn't take any longer than two minutes to review your profile, since people consume digital info quickly.

PERFECT PROFILE POINTERS

Now that you understand the strategy that goes into crafting a profile, let's review the code to making every second count. To write a profile effectively, you need to hit all of these must-haves.

> True first impression. The most important element of your profile is the first line, because it will determine whether your matches will continue reading. Make it compelling enough to draw them in and keep them scrolling to learn more: think about personal mottos, quotes you live by, or defining characteristics that speak to you. For example: "My life is a healthy balance between brain power and happy hour." "My life's soundtrack is always on remix." "I'm a foodie but not a snob." The body of your profile can go on to explain this statement. Note that a short first sentence is best, too. If it's particularly audacious, follow it up with something more low-key to balance out the intensity.

> Avoid adjective abuse. Many singles rely on weak adjectives to fill their profiles—"funny," "smart," "sophisticated," "laid-back," "nice." When someone doesn't know you, these are only vague indicators of who you are, and most people use these adjectives, so you're not making yourself stand out. Remove laundry lists, and focus on being specific about y-o-u.

> Be specific. The more precise places, activities, and parts of your lifestyle that you can include, the easier it will be for your matches to relate to you and click Compose. Think "spicy tuna rolls" over "sushi" and "racquetball" over "working out." Sneak in at least a few local hangouts so your matches can further gauge your taste level and bond with you over favorites.

❭ Present day, present tense. Steer clear of too many "way back when" stories (for example, long descriptions of your life that begin with sentences such as "I grew up in the Midwest but moved around a lot," or "I went to college in Pennsylvania but always rooted for our home team"). While it's nice to tell your matches a bit about where you come from, your profile is not an autobiography. It's more important to focus on the real-time you.

❭ Be a tease. Dating profiles are meant to intrigue your match, so don't tell your entire history—leave them with a little mystery. Talking about multiple topics and providing some information will inspire others to ask questions, which means you'll find more emails in your inbox.

❭ Exude confidence. Let's face it, confidence is sexy. Online, you can inject sex appeal into your profile through words rather than demeanor. But be careful; there's a fine line between cocky and confident. Sweeping claims like, "I'm the best [fill in the blank] you'll ever meet" go overboard. And justifying who you are ("My friends think I'm . . .") puts it too mildly and makes it appear as if you're not comfortable in your own skin.

❭ Tell a story. Rather than telling people you're adventurous, show them. Expanding on at least one or two topics in your profile through storytelling will allow your match to get a better sense of your world. Mention the time you went cliff diving in Hawaii, did stand-up comedy in front of a live audience for the first time, or backpacked through Europe after college. Including stories in your profile will make clicking with you easier.

> **Be eVulnerable.** Baring your soul online is a no-no. (Trust me, that time you accidentally drank the water in Mexico is TMI.) But there are small ways you can make yourself vulnerable without pouring your virtual heart out. Slipping in an embarrassing yet endearing story is one easy way to do this, like revealing the fact that your friends nicknamed you Grace as a joke because you're a total klutz. Techniques like this will make you approachable and relatable.

> **Spellcheck.** Check your spelling and grammar. This cannot be emphasized enough. Not only does skimping on it make you appear less intelligent and lazy (especially since most Web browsers will even spellcheck for you), but it also suggests a lack of effort and priority toward your love life—not exactly a turn-on. Trust me, so many singles who I work with won't even communicate with people who take grammar shortcuts!

> **Lasting line.** Your last line is your final impression, so end on a strong note that will inspire someone to drop you a note. Since you're conforming to the question the site asks, the approach will vary. On IvyDate.com, the last question is "I like to make a difference in the world by," while ChristianMingle.com leaves you with "a few more things I'd like to add." Either way, keep your answer upbeat. When the question is specific, as it is on IvyDate, focus on injecting passion into your answer. In this case, try discussing a particular charity or showing a softer side. And when the question is more general, as it is on ChristianMingle, use it as an opportunity to show another side of you, like mentioning your hidden love for DJ-ing. Just be sure that you never end with "Message me," since that can come off as aggressive.

> **Don't skimp.** If your profile is so sparse that a match can't get a good handle on who you are, you'll be stuck with an empty inbox. Make sure to answer all of the questions the site asks to show you're open to the possibility of meeting someone new. The only exception is if you're on a site that asks more than ten questions. If they're optional, leave a few blank, and fill out only those that best show off your personality.

NEVER-NEGATIVE NELLIE

But beyond all this, the most important thing to keep in mind when writing your profile is to be optimistic. The law of attraction says that like attracts like. And that translates to the Winkiverse, too. Negativity attracts negativity.

Never digitize your bad experiences or jaded outlooks. Regardless of how bleak things in your love life get, when you're dating online, the only thing you have to make an impression (other than photos) are your words. Keeping a sunny demeanor is important. Here's how to turn a virtual frown upside down:

> **Don't use "don't."** Remove all language that is less than optimistic, such as "never," "not," and "unfortunately." Shift your profile into happier territory. For example, rather than describing what you *don't* want in a partner, focus on what you *do* want.

> **Ax the ex.** Don't bring your past into the present. For example, if you say you hate baggage, it probably means you have some—or at least, that's how it will appear to your match. Remain future-focused.

❯ **Write and reread.** After your profile is complete, scan it for telltale signs of dating doom and gloom. Don't be afraid to delete and inject more enthusiasm.

PUTTING YOURSELF ON DIGITAL PAPER

OK, but how do you really *write* your profile?! Actually typing words about yourself into the text box is the hardest part of self-digitizing. How do you know what to focus on, how to talk about your interests, and make sure you're sending the right virtual vibe?

I know firsthand how difficult writing about yourself can be. My client Micah wanted feedback on his digital swagger, from the first few messages he sent online to his demeanor during a first meet-up. So he "mock" dated me. But before we could get to the in-person part, I had to send over my own profile so he could wirelessly woo me. Since I was busy at the moment, I asked Jess on my staff to write my profile, but when it came time to email it over, I couldn't find the document, and I couldn't reach Jess. So I put virtual pen to paper. It was rushed, but I was satisfied with it . . . until I found Jess's version. It was immediately clear that her version of my profile trumped the one I wrote. As someone who worked with me daily and noticed things about myself that I didn't, she got me better than I did! This showed me just how important it is to get outside perspective and to know how to brainstorm about yourself.

GOT WRITER'S BLOCK? BRAINSTORM KEYWORDS

Begin your profile writing by making a list of the following:

❯ Your interests, activities, classes, trips, clubs, and associations
❯ What you do during typical and atypical weeks

> The three things you're most passionate about
> Your favorite places

Once you've put everything on-screen, think back to your "audience" or ideal match. Which of these keywords might you have in common, and what would they find most intriguing? Highlight them.

Every site asks different questions of their users, but nearly all of them begin with some version of an About. This is your place to freestyle on what makes you tick. Avoid generic statements like "I'm a guy who likes to have fun," or "I love to laugh." Most people enjoy great times and giggling, so you're not really saying anything special. Instead, use this space as a storytelling opportunity that centers on your interests. But no babbling allowed! Linger on a topic for too long—more than two or three sentences—and you risk losing your match's interest.

If there's a common theme among a few of your brainstormed ideas, link them. When talking about yourself, it's best to be cohesive from start to finish and not change topics abruptly. This makes your profile stand out from more generic profiles on the site. Identifying interests or passions that can be woven throughout a few paragraphs works best.

Some sites will let you title your profile with a Headline. So after you write your About, reuse the brainstormed keywords to create a Headline. Since your Headline shows up beside your main photo in search results, it's best to tease your matches with a snippet of what they'll learn in your profile. Avoid personal-ad clichés like "Looking for Love!!!" and keep it personal. For example, if your profile focuses on the high-energy adventures and activities that fill your days, try "Bundle of Energy Enclosed."

To give you a clearer idea of what I mean, let's take a look at Mark's profile before and after his eMakeover. Full disclosure: Mark is my ex. It could be awkward to find out that your ex-girlfriend from Match.com is an online dating coach, but to Mark, it was fascinating. And now my ex-boyfriend is a client. (In fact, I've helped three of my exes date online so far!)

When I clicked on Mark's profile for the first time, I was overcome with déjà vu. I mean, ten years ago, I eFlirted with this same exact username under completely different circumstances. But his virtual pickup lines hadn't evolved since he'd wooed me a decade ago. And what once sounded so new and fresh in my teens suddenly seemed tired and boring:

I think my friends would say I'm kind and intelligent. My career is important to me, so I have goals in life that I want to accomplish. But I'm not rushing through anything. I'm lucky to have great friendships—the people in my life are definitely a priority. I like being social and enjoy meeting up for drinks. But I'm happy staying in and cooking, too. Staying fit is important to me, and so are healthy meals, so I spend a lot of time in the kitchen.

I don't have a particular type, but I find intelligence attractive. Most of all, I simply need someone who is a good person.

On the surface, you might not think that there is anything hugely wrong with Mark's profile—it's not vulgar, condescending, or too in-your-face. But it *is* drab and generic. This could be *any* man. The only thing that would inspire a match to reach out to him would be his hottie photos. Not only does this immediately limit his options, but it's risky for a guy living in a world where women typically write few messages. To make sure Mark didn't stay in the photo-only category, I rewrote his profile:

I'm not your average Spartan fan. I'm as happy about finding a great pair of Diesel jeans as I am about tailgating. Daily runs along the Hudson are as important as winning against Penn State, and a blackjack-filled Vegas trip balances out all my afternoons BBQing with the guys.

I've had an entrepreneurial spirit since I was ten. Over the years, I graduated from my neighborhood lawn-mowing business to founding a successful Internet marketing company (but I still use my green thumb in my garden). Regardless of my bottom line, my family always comes first. We're in different time zones, and I fly between JFK and SFO as often as possible.

I'm looking for a caring woman who's most comfortable hanging at home with a comedy and a bottle of wine and is never at a loss for words during an intelligent conversation. She'd be outgoing socially, with a hint of wit. If you can handle a grill, we'll definitely hit it off.

Not only is his new profile copy much different, but it also sends stronger messages and contains much more subtlety. He's still fit, social, family-oriented, and business-minded, but his profile is presented in a way that allows for a more complete depiction of his life and personality.

Mark's profile also ends with a description of his match. Although this section is supposed to be all about *you,* describing your match in a short paragraph shows that you're serious about meeting someone. This is necessary on all sites but is especially something you should focus on when you're not asked for your digi-date's details later.

MENTION YOUR MATCH
The best way to show that you're serious about meeting potential mates is to bring them up early on in your profile. Although

some sites don't ask what you're looking for until the last question, adding a brief description of your match to the end of your About section keeps the focus on dating. Just don't overdo it—mentioning your match in more than one question when you're not prompted to will seem desperate. Follow these do's and don'ts to make sure you discuss your match in an attractive way:

> **Keep it light.** Even though you're answering a heavy question, don't get too deep. Focus on how he or she might fit into your life rather than preaching political preferences or discussing morality issues. Also, limit the adjectives you use; it's best to describe your match in terms of things you'd like to do together (learning how to cook) versus listing attributes he or she should have (professional, artsy, etc.).

> **Imply intention.** Now is the time to slip in your relationship intention: are you looking for something serious or casual? This should be communicated as an implication rather than a statement. For example, if you'd eventually like to have a family, mention that you're looking for someone family-oriented rather than saying outright that you want babies.

> **Three-peat.** Look at the three characteristics you brainstormed in chapter 2 (your mate traits), and make sure they're reflected here. Weave them into the copy in an interesting way, rather than making them must-haves. For example, if it's important that your match be spontaneous, include a sentence about some out-of-the-box things you'd like to do together, such as going on a road trip without a destination in mind.

> **Avoid ultimatums.** Demanding that your match be a certain way is a negative way of approaching love or lust. Don't say things like "I am only looking for . . ." or "Please only message me if . . ." Think more along the lines of "I'd love to meet . . ." Positivity is key.

> **Remove the creep factor.** Always refer to your matches as "he" or "she." Using "you" can come off creepy, as if you're peering through their webcams unbeknownst to them. It's also an indicator of low expectations, implying that you're not picky and will go out with any "you" who might be reading. Present tense has a similar effect. Saying "she's," rather than "she'd be," can come off as assuming—after all, you're still looking for her (or him)!

DIGITAL FREE FORM

If you're known for your creativity, don't be afraid to conceptualize when you digitize. Profiles don't always need to be so straightforward. Ultimately, you want to show off what makes you unique. My client Jake was an eclectic Brooklynite who was equal parts DJ, techie, and teacher. To show off all sides of him in an interesting way, I used music as a theme throughout the text:

> Music connects the moments of my life like a soundtrack. I go from Monday morning rush hour (AC/DC, "Highway to Hell") to inspiring youth about video production (Tiesto, "Just Be") to an invigorating call from a fellow graphic designer (M.I.A., "Paper Planes"). I'm a Jets, Yankees, and Knicks fan in the evenings (Frank Sinatra, "New York, New York") . . . but don't worry, I'm Giants and Mets friendly.

You can find me playing around with the latest tech gadget *Wired* is talking about, sharing Spotify playlists with friends, or writing, writing, writing. My mind is constantly whirring. The feeling of accomplishing something is priceless to me—even if it's as mundane as syncing my iTunes playlist to my phone. While I'm a doer, I definitely daydream about getting a short story published, traveling more often, and designing my own radio station—goals for this year. But to me, life is also about the little things like injecting silliness into the day or catching up with my college buddies over a beer.

I'm looking for a woman who appreciates spontaneity, thinks big, and has an inquisitive approach to life. She should be creative and sarcastic . . . and will get extra points if she geeks out over gadgets (Lupe Fiasco, "Superstar").

BRINGING YOUR WORKPLACE INTO THE FLIRT PLACE

Almost all sites ask for a description of your job. A significant part of our life is spent in the workplace, so it's important to nail this one. Some people weigh the job section more heavily than others when viewing potential matches, but at a minimum, you can expect that your click mate will be judging you on confidence and character. The language you use will indicate where you stand professionally by coming off as either complacent, confident, or conceited. And conclusions about your character can be drawn from the pride you take (or lack) in your work.

> **eFlirt Byte:** A University of Michigan study
> shows that seven out of ten couples report that
> money causes tension in their relationship.

With a stat like that, it's no surprise that the job description is something I notice most singles prioritize when viewing profiles. But, the most important rule is that no résumé-speak is allowed! This is a dating site, not a networking opportunity. Skip your business bio, and keep things short and personal.

While Carter's intentions were in the right place when he came to me, his job section needed some work. Here's what he wrote:

> I'm a tech entrepreneur and investor. During college, I started Carter Bros. Inc., which is now a multimillion-dollar firm.

Clearly, Carter has a lot going on in his career, but it's vital to be careful about the information you put into a public profile.

Company names can easily be Googled, allowing users to dig into your life and make snap judgments (particularly if your family name is in the company name). Everything in your profile should enhance the impression you're giving your match but shouldn't be an exact description, the way a LinkedIn profile would be.

Buzzwords can create an image that is pixelated. For some, "investor" can conjure up shark-like behavior (not ideal for a potential love) or can cause matches to reach out to you for the wrong reasons (like capital for their own venture). But the bigger problem is that it's general, so if you don't back it up with a description, it lacks meaning. If you slip in a buzzword, make sure a description follows.

Dollars should never be mentioned in your profile. Whether in the Job section, the About section, or elsewhere, mentioning money is a huge no-no. It can come across as flashy and sometimes even tacky. Keeping these things in mind, let's take a look at Carter's revised job description:

I'm the CEO of a medical eCommerce company that I founded in college, and now we have five offices nationwide. It's really awesome to directly affect so many people's lives and the economy. I'm also on the board of a nonprofit and invest in companies that help Third World countries acquire technology for schools.

With Carter's new profile, we're sending the following key messages:

Success is important for an entrepreneur to highlight so it doesn't seem as if you're trying to hide the fact that in reality you're a "starving artist." Since Carter's company is so large, we replaced "entrepreneur" with "CEO" to demonstrate success. His transition from college to now is powerful, but rather than name-dropping, we explain what the company does. And instead of focusing on dollars, we mention staff. The implications are much more positive: he's providing economic stimulation through jobs instead of appearing money-hungry.

Passion is powerful, so if you're stoked about your career, show it. Carter mentioned his accomplishments before but didn't expand on what they meant to him. This is one way to personalize your career path and avoid résumé jargon.

Empathy was a great trait about Carter that was missing from his original description: he cares about the world. Volunteering his time to sit on a board shows a different side of his personality, as does investing in Third World countries. Taking "investor" out of the first sentence, moving it to the last, and combining it with a more specific form of financing paints an entirely different—and more specific—image.

Some career descriptions need finesse. To be date-friendly, some official job titles should be reworded, especially when your career isn't simple to describe. Whether you're between jobs, you're going back to school, or you lack passion when seated in your cubicle, get your iPad out, because this meeting is in session.

〉 Freelance. While you're paving your own way, working as a freelancer can raise red flags about legitimacy. Some may unfairly interpret this as code for "unemployed," "aspiring," or "unhappy." Exude passion on paper by explaining a bit about what you've accomplished so far, and include your job title. Whether it's filmmaker, consultant, or journalist, it will legitimize your career. Throwing in an impressive milestone or two will also give your match a better idea of your day-to-day.

〉 C-suite. If you're an accomplished exec, make sure your job description is just nondescript enough that your organization isn't recognized. Carter's new career description is a good example. "Medical eCommerce" is vague enough that he won't be singled out. Until you know your matches and their intentions better, only include your position and a personal line about why you enjoy it.

〉 Tricky titles. Some job titles alone can often prove challenging. Whether the title is long, is confusing, lacks an industry context, or doesn't accurately depict your expertise, the last thing you want to do is send your match Googling. If you're concerned about your title, focus on responsibilities instead. Be sure to stay away from technical terms—as long as matches have an idea of what you do, it shouldn't deter them from clicking for more info.

〉 Unemployed. Let's face it, when you're being compared with other members, government assistance isn't the biggest turn-on. Job seekers have two options: fill this section with passions, projects, and volunteer work, or leave it blank. On most sites, you'll be able to choose your industry from a drop-down list so your professional past and/or interests can still be represented. If a match is curious, he or she will ask, so be prepared to discuss your job status via email or on dates.

> **Higher ed.** Many adults decide to head back to college for an advanced degree. But without explaining your sabbatical for your higher education properly, this admirable goal could turn into a red flag regarding your earning potential as a partner. Include some background information, and focus on the ambition behind your desire to follow your dreams. The more passion you exude, the more your match will be excited, too! Remember that education should reflect your ambition, so communicate that through your description.

> **Out of the box.** I've come across a few singles who prefer to leave their careers out of their profiles altogether. I recommend doing this only if you have an obvious challenge. For example, Marni is a psychic. She uses her third eye for good, to consult executives on decision making and relationship building. In fact, she's even aided higher-ups in the government. But when she included "psychic" in her profile, her inbox grew silent. Instead, we used the same job description but replaced "psychic" with "consultant." While it's a generalization, it legitimizes an easily misinterpreted niche.

Regardless of how high a roller you are or how all-consuming your work is in your life, keep professional talk contained in the Job section unless it proves another point about your character. Otherwise, you risk taking too much focus away from your personal life. However, on the off chance that the dating site you joined doesn't give you space to talk about your career, slip it into your About section to qualify your digi-date potential. Weave it in casually, and be sure not to lead with it.

DON'T TAKE PROFILE QUESTIONS AT FACE VALUE

Sometimes the questions that online dating sites ask aren't as simple as the About or Job sections. If it's something you're uncomfortable answering or your response seems generic, try to approach it from a different angle. Here are three of my favorite tricky questions—and what you should *really* be asking yourself to make your answer a fun reflection of who you are.

The most private thing I'm willing to admit here (OkCupid .com). Forget revealing your foot fetish or number of sexual partners; the point of this question is *not* to send your matches running for the hills. Avoid giving too much information, and use this section to come off approachable by focusing on a quirk or two. Ask yourself: *What makes me unique?* Frame your response in an endearing way, and this digital bit should humanize you. For example: "I'm a coffee nerd, so my kitchen looks like a java chemistry lab."

My past relationships (JDate.com). This section can easily turn into a digital downer. Keep the ex bashing out of your profile by sharing the positive takeaways from your past relationships. Ask yourself: *What have I learned?* This will showcase positive vibes, a thoughtful attitude, and a lack of baggage. Plus, it will allow you to be a little eVulnerable. For example: "I'm independent but have learned it's OK to lean on your partner. Connecting all the way can't happen if you're holding back."

Five things you can't live without (eHarmony.com). It's easy to fill this section with basics such as friends, family, and your laptop, but if you can be unique, you are less likely to lose your matches when they get to this section. Skip the assumed, and use this as a place to showcase the real you. Ask yourself: *What specifics in life are my favorites?* For example, my five would be iced chai lattes, the Whitney Museum, peep-toe heels, Amtrak quiet car writing sessions, and Central Park picnics.

LEAVE NO QUESTION BOX UNCHECKED

While the free-write sections allow you to show off your clever self, don't underestimate the value of the site's other profile features, like checking off your favorite types of exercise.

> eFlirt Byte: POF users who list more than ten interests see a 50-percent increase in messages.

While sites vary, one thing almost all of them have in common is the Interests section. This allows you to indicate your lifestyle preferences in a variety of categories like "dining out," "tennis," or "music." This is often how singles will find you, by filtering further and viewing those who not only fit their specs but also indicate a penchant for, say, hiking.

SHOW SUBSTANCE, BUT ALLOW FOR SKIM-ABILITY

Regardless of how perfectly worded your profile is, not every match will read it in its entirety. A study by Jakob Nielsen, an expert in online usability, used eye-tracking software to determine that online users read only 28 percent of the text on a Web page. And on a similar note, mobile usage is overtaking desktop Internet trolling.

> eFlirt Byte: Microsoft Tag's study on mobile marketing found that 50 percent of all local searches are done from a cell phone.

With a smaller screen, singles viewing on their mobiles have even shorter attention spans, and skimming is the norm. This means that the buzzwords you do use should pop just as much on an iPhone as on a MacBook Pro.

But all of this does not mean you should write less. Quite the opposite: construct short paragraphs, use lists, and incorporate keywords to ensure that you stand out. While job buzzwords should be avoided in your profile, interest buzzwords can be an asset. Seeing things such as "travel" or "cooking" during a skim-through will make your match feel that you have enough in common to warrant an email and, perhaps, a full read-through of your profile.

GRAMMAR RULES ALWAYS RULE

Beyond your words, it's important to maintain proper profile etiquette. When words on a cyber-page are your first impression, it's easy to rub your match the wrong way inadvertently. Avoid these profile missteps to keep grammar sexy.

> **Ellipses craze.** One or two ellipses are fine, but going crazy with them changes the tone of your profile. Using too many in midsentence draws your profile out, making it much longer for no reason, while ending with them sounds ominous . . .

> **DIGITAL SCREAM.** Writing in all caps is a major turn-off. Whether it's to prove a point in a particular phrase or the entire style of your profile, it will appear as if you're not technologi-

cally advanced and don't know any eCommunication etiquette. And if you're not privy to proper online communication, it might be challenging for a match to believe that you understand dating communication, not to mention that you can come off, well, angry.

> **Running on and on and on and on.** Separating your words into paragraphs isn't just grammatically correct; it also allows users to skim your profile more easily. Most matches won't read every word of your profile, so creating text that the eye can easily navigate will help you get the most click-throughs to your inbox.

> **Exclaim-aholic.** Exclamation points can help move the energy forward and inject passion, but limit your profile to one per section. Too much enthusiasm can read as disingenuous. Men should be even more sparing with their use, since this punctuation form can make you come off as too feminine and excitable.

> **Perma-smile.** Too many emoticons in your profile can seem juvenile and forced. Ladies, one wink or smile should be the max. Men, eliminate them completely—winky faces just aren't masculine.

> **Lower-case addiction.** Typing in all lower-case is not only a grammar-police offense, but it also makes it very challenging to read through and skim your profile. Although you may be aiming for a casual tone, it will likely leave your match questioning your education level—or just exasperated.

When you're on more than one dating site, be savvy when reusing the same profile. I worked with Anan on two of his profiles, but the second was exactly the same as the first. And I do mean exactly—he copy-and-pasted all of the cool questions and answers from one site into his About section on another. It looked as if he'd decided to interview himself, and it raised a red flag, since it was obvious that he was answering questions from another site.

While you can use what you've written on one site for another, you need to adjust to the site's settings so that others in the community will find you digitally dashing. Leverage parts of your original profile, but you'll inevitably have to come up with some new material to make your profile pop off the screen. Don't worry about people seeing duplicate information about you between platforms; if they're on the same two sites, it will look consistent, not desperate, just like you might have a similar bio on two social media sites.

Regardless of all the ins and outs of creating a profile, remember while you're typing that you're more than the sum of these few words. This is a snapshot of your life, not a definition. And, like life, your profile is a work in progress that can easily change. While you may be putting your heart on the line (quite literally), it's only the beginning of your online dating story. Once you put the final period on your profile, don't overthink. Hit submit, and starting flirting!

Email Education

FLIRTING THROUGH INBOXES

Winking is dead. No, not the real-life eye fluttering, but the button you'll find next to someone's profile that allows you to show interest in a match. Some sites call it Smiling or Flirting, but regardless it serves the same purpose: to let you gauge interest in someone before investing hours poring over every period of a single clever email sent to their inbox.

Years ago, when dating sites first entered the scene, Winking was all the rage. But it has become an increasingly passive action. Consider this: if a Facebook "friend" you've never met face-to-face "liked" your status update, would it inspire you to write a detailed email in return? I think not. Needless to say, your first interaction with a clickable mate is often your make-or-break moment and should *not* come by way of a generic emoticon. It's unlikely that it will inspire any action . . . in your inbox or otherwise.

The truth is that women can *sometimes* still get away with merely clicking the Wink button—especially hotties with bodies. But if you're truly interested in a match, you shouldn't blow your one opportunity with a seemingly meaningless attempt. Isn't your future partner worth a few sentences?!

Of course, the most important reason to ignore Winking online and leave it only to real-life scenarios is "mat-uration," the sat*uration* of *mat*ches like you on a site. The number of singles dating online is growing every day, which means that more and more conversation is happening. You want to make sure that you're an active participant so you don't get lost in the shuffle and miss an opportunity with a match simply because his or her inbox is flooded and Winks are automatically deleted. (Trust me, singles do it.) In fact, many eDaters are even savvy enough to spot a generic, template message and get rid of them without so much as a response.

To be truly proactive and productive in your digital dating life, you have to click Compose and start typing a message tailored specifically for your cyber-crush's eyes only. There are four phases of sending messages: first messages, email replies, transitioning offline, and following up. But each needs to be approached differently; let's break it down.

First Emails

Sending a first-email flirtation has three purposes:

1. Get a match's attention. Technology should always work for you, not against you. But the truth is that with so many potential matches online, it's possible that Mr. or Ms. Right (or Right Now) might not come across your profile. Maybe your profile doesn't make a cameo until page 10 of their search results. If they sign off after viewing only five pages, they'll miss you entirely. What you're saying at the most basic level when you send an email is "I exist, listen up!"

2. Qualify yourself. Vouching for yourself as a qualified match is important. So even though you've already created a profile, you want to rehash what makes you a clickable mate for them. Avoid pleas ("If you like what you saw on my profile, too, message me back") and basics ("I'm a well-educated, charming, and funny guy looking for a woman like you"), and qualify yourself more naturally by mentioning an interest or two that you share.

3. Start a conversation. Remember that messaging takes two—if you don't begin chatting, you'll never get offline. Encourage conversation and responses by writing an email meant specifically for him or her, and then ask a question. Questions show that you have genuine interest in getting to know someone and really begin the conversation.

Applying all three of these criteria creates email perfection. But deciding what to write once you click Compose isn't always as clear-cut or straightforward.

Getting responses to the emails you send starts with reading your match's profile.

Just as you may experience love at first sight in person, a similar tug at your heartstrings could happen when viewing a match's pictures. But just because someone's photos are swoon-worthy doesn't mean you should skip the rest of their profile—you might be missing out on some vital information (or even a red flag or two). You'll also get to know specifics about your common interests that you can talk or ask more about, showing this digital cutie that yes, you cared enough to read through the profile, making it more likely that you'll get a response.

But there will also be cases when someone just seems *right* for you, even though you can't put your fingertip on what makes that person your "type." It might be his or her sense of style, the tone of the About section, or simply one funny sentence that literally made you LOL. And that's when crafting an email that qualifies yourself and starts a conversation can clinch permanent space on his or her heart's hard drive.

If it's not immediately apparent how you'll click, ask yourself: *What do I like about him or her?* This will help give your email direction. I do this exercise with Khristine during our weekly sessions. As a thirty-four-year-old New Yorker with a busy schedule, she meets with me to be held accountable for the time she commits to online dating and the decisions she makes. Her first thought about what appeals to her in someone's profile is usually along the lines of "He seems genuine." But after a few moments, she'll come up with a few others, such as "He sounds successful like me," or "I haven't read that book he mentions yet, but I really enjoyed the author's first novel." And suddenly, we have a perfect topic for her first email. Discussing how genuine someone seems is too intangible and broad a topic for a first message. And while success is fantastic, we don't want to start off a pending love connection with job talk—it's not very romantic! However, discussing favorite authors not only highlights a similar interest but also shows comparable levels of intelligence, which is important if you pride yourself on book smarts as much as Khristine does.

If you're having a hard time determining a topic for a message, look at passions and keywords.

Passions are the best topics of conversation, particularly if you have a few in common. Believe it or not, I notice that passions are not usually the focus of people's profiles. But by looking closely at language and phrasing, you can figure out what a match is excited about in life. For example, if someone mentions an organization like Habitat for Humanity, you can bet that helping others is something he or she cares deeply about. If you can tap into what people have a passion for, they'll *want* to respond. After all, when someone asks you about something you love, don't you just want to gush all about it?

Reviewing keywords doesn't require you to read between the lines the way finding a passion does, but it's a solid strategy if you're struggling to find a point of connection. Scan your match's profile for interests that you share, such as travel, yoga, or family. If he or she doesn't expand on the topic in their profile, use your message as an opportunity to ask more about it, while giving insight into why that topic ranks high in your life.

INTRODUCTION TO INTRODUCTIONS

Now that you've determined a topic, let's dive into the components that make up a great email.

> **Greeting.** Since the purpose of a message is to begin a conversation, skip traditional letter etiquette. "Hello," "Yo," "Hiya," and other jargon create a more formal tone than you want to project. Hands down, the best way to begin an email is just to jump right in with no salutation at all. While it may seem strange, it creates instant familiarity, which will encourage him

or her to feel a connection. I've always seen the best results with my clients who follow this advice, and OkCupid agrees: avoiding a salutation gets the highest response rates on that site. But if skipping a salutation feels too strange to you, note that OkCupid found that "How's it going?" "What's up?" and "Howdy" ranked high as greetings in its study.

> **Content.** As you did with your profile, skip sentences that sound generic. Being specific is even more important in messages, because you want to show honest intent. If the message sounds even a little bit as if it wasn't written specifically for the recipient, you risk missing out on a reply. Ideally, you should stick to one topic so your message is focused. If there are two that go hand-in-hand, you can expand, but more than that, and you risk sounding too interested for a simple hello.

> eFlirt Byte: According to OkCupid's email study,
> every niche word or phrase the site has data
> on has a positive effect on messaging, such
> as "vegetarian," "band," and "grad school."
> And phrases that engage these interests and
> show that you've read the other person's profile
> are also likely to get responses, like "Curious
> what . . ." and "Noticed that . . ."

> **Language.** However, remember that this isn't a text message, either; you should still use proper grammar and sentence structure. Steer clear of netspeak like "ur," "ya," or "wat." Because OkCupid is a free site, I'd expect some of its members to be the most forgiving of this digital behavior, but the site's study found

it to be a strong deal breaker. However, users do respond well to humor, so "haha" and "lol" are OK.

› Question. Asking one question at the end of a message is a must. While profile "calls to action" are subtle, those in emails should be more direct. The easier you can make it for the recipient to respond, the more likely you are to get a reply. But it's just as important to make your call to action clear. Asking three questions instead of one can become overwhelming or feel like badgering, and the person might not respond at all. And keep the question simple. Elaborate inquiries require your match to give serious thought to responding and, again, can leave you with no response. Start with your experience on the topic, and then ask a simple yes-or-no question. Uncomplicated questions will encourage your match to expand on the topic.

› Subject. Most dating sites allow you to create a title for your message, which is what your match will click on in his or her inbox. Make sure it is click-worthy, and avoid generic lines like "What's Up?" or "Let's Talk." You want the title to speak to the topic so your match knows what they're clicking on. But remember that this is your dating life, not corporate life. Skip titles that are dry, such as "Cooking," and instead use something with personality, like "Battle of the Lasagnas." When your match's inbox is bursting with messages, yours will be much more likely to stand out.

› Signature. Always close the email with your name. While this might sound like a no-brainer, many singles leave it off and risk coming across as mysterious—and not in a good way. Sending a match a message means that you're introducing yourself, so make sure you do that. Plus, signing with your name instantly warms up the tone of the email. Needless to say, you should also skip any extraneous information, like a full signature with your title, email address, and phone number. Not only does this set too formal of a vibe, but it also compromises your safety.

Let's put these principles into practice. Ultimately, an email should look similar to the following:

> From: sunnysideup
> Sent: January 22 8:43 PM
> To: DownWith311
> Subject: Poker Face
> I'm a budding poker player, too. Right now, I'm reading Small Stakes Hold'em to brush up on my game. In March, I'm heading to Vegas, but quick trips to Atlantic City with friends are fun, too. Where do you play?
> Sarah

A first message should be short and sweet; there's no need to bare your soul before your match even says hi. Ideal length depends on gender, location, and age. Women should write less, usually three or four sentences—much longer, and you risk appearing overenthusiastic. Traditional gender roles dictate that men should be the aggressors, so when you do the approaching, give the guy some space to take the reins later. Men should write a bit more, but still not too much—four to ten sentences is ideal. This will show that a decent amount of time and thought went into the email. But also keep geography in mind; younger or urban singles like Sarah favor shorter messages, while more mature or suburban/rural singles often have more traditional values and want to know that you put significant effort into contacting them.

Template emails are the pickup lines of the Web.

Being proactive and sending an appropriate number of emails is important, but avoid copy-and-paste jobs—you know, template messages that are so generic you can send them to matches in bulk. They're the "How do you do's" that aren't tailored to a match and often rub people the wrong way. Approaching a cutie in real life with a cheesy line will either result in an eye roll or attract a lower-quality mate, and the same is true of the Wink Wide Web.

The first time I logged into Jonathan's inbox to assess his emails, I had to step away for some deep, cleansing breathes. He had sent everyone in the continental U.S. with *any* potential the same template message:

Youre so gorgeous, I'd fly to [fill in the blank] to see you, call me 305-555-9823 xoxo Johno

Sending the same message to every match may seem efficient, but skimping on personalized messages is actually a major time waster. If your first email is the online equivalent of a first encounter, template emails are worse than a limp handshake. Jonathan's emails epically failed, because he gave a disingenuous compliment ("gorgeous," when he'd never met her before), was overenthusiastic (saying he'd jet over ASAP), made himself seem too available (revealing his phone number), and ended with faux affection (kisses, hugs, and a nickname).

Remember, a little email foreplay is never a bad thing. But that's not what "Johno" was serving up. His messages screamed

"You're not worth getting to know more, so let's just meet offline and be inappropriate together."

The one circumstance when templates can sometimes be effective is when you're only looking to date casually, because you can increase the number of messages sent. In these cases, emails are typically shorter, and the tone is more laid-back. Take Alex, my twenty-nine-year-old client whose preference was to schedule at least three dates a week and simply have fun and see what happened. In that case, I drew up outlines that he could use in place of templates. Of course, they still required him to do some work, but he could more easily increase his output. This is OK, because over time, there are common topics you find appealing in others' profiles that you may use often to message matches. One of his big interests is travel, and most of the matches he chose had a large appetite for going abroad, too. So I created this guideline with travel as the focal point:

Looks like your travel bug is as big as mine. My favorite trip so far was the Amalfi Coast—the architecture was amazing. [Country] must have been___. I [have/haven't] been there before, [and/but]___. I have a trip to Prague and Amsterdam planned this summer, which I'm really excited about. Where are you headed next?
Alex

When creating an outline, be sure to erase signs of it being generic by remaining hyper-focused on the topic. As much as possible, remove blanket sentences that sound as if they could be sent to anyone, such as "I really enjoyed your profile."

And if you see the same match on more than one dating site, don't message in two places. Reaching out twice becomes badgering. If the person wasn't attracted to your profile from the start, there's nothing about a duplicate message that will be a turn-on. Stay focused on writing messages for new people to keep the positivity flowing in your dating life.

Email Replies

Emailing is the digital equivalent of courtship.

When my clients are online dating newbies, sometimes their first instinct is to get offline and talk on the phone immediately. This was the case for Julie, who messaged with a match once and then dropped her number, requesting that he contact her that same evening between seven and ten. But her phone never rang.

Never mind that scheduling the call was too formal (and too short notice); making the transition from first email to the phone changes the method of communication drastically before you know each other, making it more likely that singles won't follow through. And when you do this so soon, there is less incentive to call, because they still don't know much about you.

It's important to get comfortable with cyber chatter, because it's part of courting someone in a 2.0 world. Skipping straight to the phone means you miss out on the natural development of a dynamic. As a result, phone calls and dates might seem forced, and connecting with someone when you're offline can be more challenging.

But if you're asked to chat voice-to-voice early on and you really like the person, go ahead and follow his or her lead if you're comfortable with it. Even though it's best to eCourt each other, you don't want to block your eFlirting energy from moving forward—offline.

With Julie's next match, she exchanged six emails before connecting offline. This time, not only did he call, but they ended up dating for a few weeks.

Gone are three-day rules; all hail real-time gratification.
Stop wasting time debating whether you should wait until tomorrow or Tuesday to write back to your match, and *just hit Reply*. This rule is in effect always and forever, whether you're dealing with an ongoing email string or a new eFlirtation. Your goal should be to reply to a message within twenty-four hours. Do yourself a favor, and download your dating site's mobile app to help keep you on point. Just be careful of typing errors, and always reread what you've written before pushing Send so you're not a victim of auto-correct.

When you click Reply, your focus should be on remaining a good conversationalist. Just as when you're chatting in person, you want to keep the flow going and the momentum moving in a getting-to-know-you direction. This means showing interest by asking one or two questions (it's OK to ask more than one once you're both engaged in chatter) and expanding on questions about yourself. But keep your responses to no longer than one paragraph per topic.

Here's a message string between Kyle, a twenty-nine-year-old teacher in Boston, and his latest lady. Let's see firsthand how a great relationship starts via email.

From: openpassport
Sent: January 7 5:28 PM
To: beachesandtoes
Subject: China Vacay
One of your photos reminded me of my trip to China. I went with

a friend, and we explored Mt. Taishan, one of the Five Sacred
Mountains— an eye-opening experience. The best dumplings I
ever had were by a chef nicknamed "Elton John" in my friend's
rural village. What was your trip to Asia like?
Kyle

———————

Hi Kyle,
Glad you liked my photo. The waterfall I photographed was
actually at Mt. Taishan, too. I went to China about two years ago
and had a fascinating time, though wasn't lucky enough to run
into Elton. ;)
I actually just got back from Chicago tonight—just in the nick
of time, since snow seems to be looming. But what else is new!
Maybe you'll get a snow day tomorrow. What grade do you teach?
Tanya

———————

Hey Tanya,
I just got in from a huge workout that I'm officially dubbing the
Snow Shoveling Marathon.
Luckily I got the "no school" call last night. I teach fifth grade,
which is interesting because the kids are at that age where
they're just starting to learn the definition of a crush.
I'm glad you made it out of Chicago before all the airports closed.
Being stuck somewhere is right up there with breaking a bone
on my continuum of life experiences. Tough time of year to be in
Chicago—were you there for business or fun?
Kyle

———————

Hey Kyle,
Fifth grade, how cool! For me, that was the prime note-passing age.
I was in Chicago for fun—actually, it was a girlfriend's bachelorette party! The best part by far was our dinner at Wildfire. Best. Steak. Ever. Have you ever been there? Let me tell you, after the weekend we had, I'm on an official wine detox!
Tanya

Hey Tanya,
I haven't been to Wildfire but will have to add it to my list of to-do's next time I'm in Chi-town. Steakhouses are a favorite. I'd love to continue chatting offline—maybe we can make snow angels and then warm up with a hot chocolate. I hear whipped cream is the new detox. When are you free this week?
Kyle

Hey Kyle,
How fun! A hot chocolate and some snow-angel workouts sound exactly like what my system needs. ;) I'm free Saturday or Sunday afternoon. Let me know which works better!
Tanya

Hey Tanya,
Saturday is great. Let's meet at 2 PM in front of Thinking Cup, and then we can head over to the Boston Common together.

In case anything changes (and so we can find each other), my number is 781-555-2387. Looking forward to meeting you! :-)
Kyle

Awesome! See you then. My cell is 617-555-9831.
Tanya

Kyle is one of my success stories; he's now in a relationship, and I couldn't be prouder of his eFlirting skills. Every time a client like him emails telling me that he or she is seeing someone seriously, I blush from head to stiletto from the thanks—I can't help feeling the love radiating off the computer screen.

Every email exchange is different, meaning that "rules" can't truly exist; however, there *are* nuances that can be learned from Kyle and Tanya's connection:

❯ **Hi, hello, hey.** Kyle followed my advice on first messages to a T. His initial email not only reads well and is interesting, but clearly, it caught Tanya's eye. When she responded, she said "Hi." Good but not great. "Hi" is a little formal for flirting territory, but when Kyle followed up, he said "Hey." And then she followed his lead. Small word choices like this will help create a more comfortable cyber-environment and help you get offline for a date.

❯ **Conversation versus content.** Kyle successfully mixed new information about himself with casual conversation. He related well to her and showed interest by asking questions, but he also added enough details about his own life to keep the momentum moving. When one person drops off the email string, it's usually because the right mix of both elements is missing. Remember: relate, then add.

> **One question per paragraph.** You don't want to overwhelm someone with questions, so stick to one per paragraph. This will to force you to include content alongside your inquiries.

> **Emoticons.** In the first email Tanya sent, she Winked. This is always a good sign from a lady—digital flirtation at its finest. But Kyle waited until the last email to smile. In a male-female situation, this is the right approach. Although it may sound strange to advise men not to reciprocate a virtual smiley, emoticons typically give off energy that isn't as confident—as if you have to justify your statement, even though the real purpose is to show excitement. Avoid them until the end of an online string, since that's where you want to convey more genuine emotion and excitement; that way, it shows that your virtual Wink is the real deal.

> **Number-drop.** Even if you're not going to talk on the phone first, dropping your digits is important. It almost always encourages the other person to reciprocate. This way, if one person is running late or you're in a crowded space and are having trouble recognizing each other, you can be in touch.

> **Creative date ideas.** Planning a date beyond cocktails can make your match feel special; just make sure that it jives with the discussion you've had so far. Kyle and Tanya's conversation centered around the snow storm and her need for a wine detox. Suggesting that they take advantage of the weather and indulge

in a virgin beverage is not only unique (it's unlikely that she'll have this date with anyone else), but it also shows that he can fit into her lifestyle.

MESSAGING MISHAPS

When you're composing responses to your suitors, remember that there are some topics of conversation you should avoid:

❯ **Sex.** Even if you're seeking a casual relationship, putting your bedroom etiquette out there too soon can set the virtual vibe that you'd rather skip the actual date. Unless you're specifically looking for a no-strings-attached relationship and your only aim is nookie, skip the virtual sexy time.

❯ **Religion.** The first few emails are not the time to mention (or ask about) religion. Unless you're on a niche dating site geared to a specific religion, it's too soon to dive into such heavy territory. Your theories on heaven and hell can come later.

❯ **Past relationships.** Beginning a new relationship by referring to an old one starts things on a sour note. It's unlikely that your match will want to get involved with you if it sounds like you're hung up on an ex.

❯ **Marriage.** If your ultimate goal is to tie the knot, that's something to keep in mind as you date online but should not be focused on in emails. It's getting too many steps ahead of yourself. Keep conversation light and fun until the relationship develops more offline.

〉 Oh-so-personal moments. There are things in life that are best kept as close memories until the right time comes to discuss them. I'm not suggesting that you lie, just that you avoid more personal matters, such as deaths in the family or health issues, when chatting online. It may seem natural to reveal the details of your dad's death when your match asks if you're close to your family, but unloading too much emotional baggage or putting your match in a must-empathize position will make the scenario awkward, even if you didn't mean it to. Save these topics for offline once the relationship has developed.

〉 Children. If you have kids, you should absolutely state it in your profile by ticking the correct box. But unless your children have something in common with a match's kids (gleaned from his or her profile, of course), there's no reason to bring up your family. The focus of your email string should be the two of you, so you can get to know each other better and develop a rapport. Discussing your twelve-year-old's soccer leagues won't achieve that.

〉 Politics. Whether you lean to the left or the right, these details should be kept for later. If you're passionate about the topic or volunteer for a party, include that in your profile, but avoid mentioning it in emails. Putting where you stand out there is one thing, but discussion has potential to shift you into debate territory, which can rub one (or both) of you the wrong way before you even meet in person.

eFlirt Byte: According to a study by the
University of Miami, only 14 percent of singles
even bothered to check off their political

interests in their profile preferences. It ranked twenty-third out of twenty-seven interest categories—just below video games.

When you encounter a mute match, lead by example.
Occasionally, you'll attempt chitchat with a match of few virtual words. Remember that not everyone is as confident as you. Lead by example: the more you write, the more you should get back. If your initial message to your match was three lines, and he or she responds with one, make sure that your next email is a bit longer, say, seven sentences. Also, switch strategies and ask an open-ended question rather than something that can be answered with a yes or a no. If this doesn't lead to more discussion, ditch the conversation. If a match isn't willing to converse on the Web in more than twenty words, it's unlikely that he or she will put effort into offline dating, either.

Don't break up with someone before you even say hello.
Not all emails are created equal. There will inevitably be matches that enter your inbox whom you'd rather avoid. When someone you don't see potential with crosses your monitor, it's OK not to engage. While it may sound harsh, there's no need to respond unless you want to.

In the dial-up days, it was standard to respond to each and every message with a "Thanks, but no thanks." But while responding this way might seem like the nice thing to do, it can often bring out the worst in people. Against my advice, Sage sent her match a "Thanks, but no thanks" note, and this is what he wrote back:

From: RomanticCynicNYC
Sent: August 19 3:21 PM
To: beingeve
Subject: RE: Favorite Spots
Well, why?! The site says we're a 98% match. I'm not just some short, lame guy, I'm a good guy. Why won't you go out with me? Whatever, forget it. Good luck with some dumb jock because that's the only thing you'll be able to get. You're not even worth typing this. Honestly if you think you're a 10 you've got to be joking. Max 5. I can do way better. Good luck with those horse teeth.

She was close to tears when she called me after reviewing this blow to her single gal ego. I advised her not to respond and to hit the Block button (although the horse teeth comment made her self-conscious for months).

If a match is mean, immediately block.
There are few instances when you should block a match. If you simply didn't jive with someone offline but consider him or her a good person, there's no reason to get Block-button happy unless this person is badgering you. But when people flare their digital nostrils and get mean, make sure they're on your short list of people who can never contact you again.

To avoid negative nellies, only respond to matches you're not into if they write particularly long and thought-out messages based on your profile. People who put a significant amount of thought into messaging you will likely be more hurt by silence. Engaging in conversation brings false hope and allows them the opportunity to lash out. If you *do* feel the need to respond, keep it simple. Thank them for the messages, mention that you don't think that you're the right match, and, of course, end by wishing them well.

Transitioning Offline

The ultimate success of online dating is going on awesome dates and, if you're looking for something serious, a relationship. But that won't happen unless you get offline. Your opinions of your match might shift when you see each other's facial expressions and body language. You'll either develop chemistry on a more personal level—or not.

Take things beyond the broadband and meet up after six messages total. After you've written three emails to your match, it's time to get offline—any more, and you risk creating an entirely Web-based relationship. Six is enough to get comfortable with each other and should leave you wanting to know more. But men and women tackle these situations differently, so let me break it down by gender.

GENTS

Women *want* to be asked out. Trust me. Shy-guy routines don't translate to the Web, so simply ask her out. Since you've already communicated back and forth, it's unlikely she'll reject you at this late stage, so you should be confident in yourself when sending this final email.

The difference between asking a woman out in person and doing so online is in the phrasing. In fact, you don't ask. Write her a normal, conversational email, and end with a statement about meeting up. Then ask when works best for her. Kyle used this technique.

This formula continues the trend of making it easy for your match to click Reply. But more important, it projects confidence, which can often get lost when you're hiding behind a laptop.

LADIES

I know it's not ideal to ask a guy out, but remember that online dating is an entirely new way of wooing. Men don't always know how to ask you out (or if they do, they might be too scared to ask). Even though online communication seems black-and-white, there are still a lot of gray areas. So don't be afraid to take matters into your own hands.

Although the rules for guys can work for you, too, keep in mind that there can be some differences. For example, you can skip the six-message rule if your messages are more in-depth and you're spending more than five minutes to compose a response. In some cases, requesting to meet might happen during your second message rather than your third.

But if you're not comfortable being the one requesting a date, nudging him to ask you out should work like a charm. Here are three ways to give him a virtual signal that all systems are go:

1. Mention something current. It's cool that you bonded over your favorite museums from your profiles. But in order to meet in person, you need to remind him that you're here and now, not merely an online pen pal. Mention a current art exhibit, what you've heard about it, and that you'd love to check it out. Then ask if he's been. Hopefully he'll mention that you should head to the museum—or whatever activity you're discussing—together.

2. Bring up the weekend. Mentioning the weekend is a surefire way to get your match thinking about asking you out; talking about life's happenings offline reminds him that moving things along with you means meeting in person. Ask what he's up to during his time off, hoping that he'll respond with his plans and the possibility of including you in them—even if it ends up being for Monday. Most first online dates take place after work, which will encourage him to include you in his plans the following week.

3. Be bold. If all else fails, you'll have to be digitally daring. When subtle hints don't work, simply say that you'd love to meet. The trick here is to make it a statement, not a question. That way, when he responds, he can officially ask you out.

Regardless of your gender, if your match says that he or she will be out of town, has a serious deadline, or anything else that signals preoccupation, keep the conversation going in the meantime. Just be sure to ask him or her out when the busy spurt winds down. If there is some lag time between your last message and date night, don't feel the need to fill the void with chatter. Once you set up the date, there's no reason to keep in touch until you get offline—unless, of course, it's to confirm plans. So nix any random texts or messages without a purpose. Your next connection should be face-to-face.

PHONE VERSUS MEET-UP

Remember that everyone has his or her own preferences, too. Don't be caught off-guard if a match asks to talk on the phone before meeting up. People have different comfort levels with meeting people they encounter online. In urban areas, singles typically prefer to meet without chatting on the phone, and in fact, I usually recommend skipping that step. If you both lead busy lives, it can become challenging to catch each other for a conversation and become yet another barrier to connecting. While spending more time on email and on the phone can help develop the relationship, it also can be a waste of time, because the only way to truly connect is to meet offline.

Gail messaged with Stewart for a week before they got offline, and by then, I could tell that she was infatuated with him. She owns a fashion company and enjoys evenings at the symphony. So she was turned on by his duality as a hedge-fund partner and a violinist. When he sent her recordings from his recent recital, her enthusiasm seemed to double. But even though they chatted on the phone, all of that chemistry disappeared on their date—the mutual-attraction factor simply wasn't there. It's easy to build someone up in your mind before you meet, so pump the brakes until you get in person.

There will be times when an email string will leave you feeling iffy about your match's potential. In cases like this, the phone is your best tool. Suggest chatting on the phone if you're on the fence about your compatibility. Keep the call around ten minutes, which should be plenty of time to determine whether a date would be wise.

Remember that emailing with matches never obliges you to meet them. If you're not feeling it at any point in your email string, kindly bow out. First, go silent on your email string. If they persist and begin pestering your inbox with multiple messages, mention that you've enjoyed chatting but are speaking with someone else right now—which you are! Communicating with other matches simultaneously is necessary. But in the context of this email exchange, mentioning as much is a polite yet definitive way of discontinuing the convo. It's important that you don't waste your time—or theirs.

Emails create touch points for date conversation.

Remember, the ultimate reason to email with potential dates is to get a sense of each other's personality and to develop a bond. Although email exchanges may seem trivial, they actually lay a foundation for relationship development and will save you from awkward silences on your dates.

When you keep this in mind, you won't feel as if you're diving off the dating deep end. Trust me, when you're sixty-three and divorced, like my client Corinne, meeting someone from the Internet can cause major first-date jitters. When she last dated, the Internet didn't even exist, never mind the notion of meeting a stranger after a few messages. To her, the Web was a place she visited exclusively for work correspondence and photos of her grandkids, not a meet market. But she knew that online was where the singles her age hung out. When she had a sudden flash of panic before her first date, she called me and ranted about how she knew nothing about the person who was about to be on the other side of her table. I calmed her by reminding her that she actually knew a lot about him from their email exchanges. And trust me, this isn't something only older singles experience. Even the most tech-savvy twenty-somethings freak out about the lack of information they feel they have about a match. When your mind goes into overdrive, remember that online dating is all about getting to know someone new and that you've chatted previously. You can refer back to email anecdotes to fill the silence and to delve deeper into what makes him or her tick.

Following Up

While it's simple to send a message off into the Winkiverse, it's not always as easy to obtain a response. But all hope is not lost if you don't hear from your match. There's a secret to the trade that not everyone knows: the follow-up message. After all, in the world of cyber-love, lots of factors can deter matches from emailing you back:

› **They're busy at the moment.** You never know what's going on in other people's lives. It's a common misconception that if someone logs on, reads your email, clicks through to your profile, and doesn't respond, it means he or she isn't interested. Not always the case! It may simply be that the person didn't have time to write you back then but might get to it later. Keep an open mind.

› **Their dating calendar is full.** Just because your match has an active profile doesn't mean he or she is actively dating. Matches may be checking messages, but their dance cards might be full. When a dating calendar gets full, matches will sometimes wait a while to respond until things cool off and they're ready (and eager) to meet someone new.

› **They don't pay.** Most paid dating sites allow all members to have profiles, but only those who pay for a subscription can message. Just because someone showed up as a match and has logged on recently doesn't mean that he or she is a full-fledged member who can reply to you.

› **You got lost.** If his or her inbox is a virtual hot spot, your message might have been buried or deleted before it was even read.

❭ Your profile wasn't good enough. If your photos were unclear or your text wasn't specific, you might not have made the cut. Hey, everyone has different preferences!

Online dating takes persistence. Of all of the scenarios above, the only real potential blow to your ego would be if your profile didn't resonate with your match; all others are the result of miscommunication or unlucky timing. Make sure you stay on the same page—literally and figuratively—by sending a follow-up to get your match's attention. Since each scenario is different, below are the three that my clients most commonly encounter and easy troubleshooting tips:

1. The 10/3 rule. If it's been more than ten days since you emailed and the match has logged on within the last three, it's OK to send a follow-up. Never send back-to-back messages without a large time lapse like this and knowing that the other person signed on recently (if that functionality is available to you)—it will seem pushy the next time he or she logs in. The goal is to keep your follow-up short and sweet, with no negativity or guilt trips. Let the match know that you're still hoping to connect. However, be prepared for it not to always go your way. Your match might respond, "Best of luck" . . . or not at all. If he or she does read it and doesn't answer within a few days, at least you have closure, and you know it wasn't simply a missed connection.

2. Revamp your stats. If it's been a while since you've updated your page, think about uploading some new photos, revising your profile, and updating your preferences before reaching out again. Refreshing your profile page can often elicit responses from matches who may have previously passed you over.

3. Disappearing act. If you were in the middle of a great email string and your match suddenly vanished, see if he or she has been online recently rather than wondering where in the World Wide Web they went to. If so and it's been more than five days since you last heard from the person, respond to the email string again and see how things are going. The lack of response was likely an accident.

Above all, don't take it personally! Jumping to conclusions will only make the online dating process more challenging.

Remember that dating is about *flirting,* and doing that over emails requires a coy tone devoid of sarcasm. Make your messages light and fun, but delete cheesy pickup lines from the screen. These don't work in person, and you won't fare much better if you're dishing them digitally.

Emailing gets you both offline. While you may feel tingles through your iPad from your match's words, experiencing that spark in person will lead to an offline relationship—no Winks necessary.

CHAPTER 5

Love Triangle 2.0

DATING MULTIPLE MATCHES

It's impossible to date effectively online without seeing multiple matches. Don't worry, I'm not suggesting that you bed-hop, but contacting only one match at a time will leave your love life heading nowhere fast. Everyone's flirting reaction time differs. Some members log on daily, others do it weekly, and some go AWOL for a while before returning. In short, you can't be assured that sending a message will elicit a timely response.

To avoid virtual crickets, send multiple messages into the Winkiverse.
If you're used to being a serial monogamist offline, dating a few people at once might seem dishonest. But having a dating queue doesn't mean you're cyber-slutty. In the online dating world, it's necessary to reach out to many people before you commit to One. Since the dating process begins more casually, it's expected that everyone is seeing other people until you become more seriously committed. But don't get hung up on what other people are doing. For now, let's focus entirely on your own digital dating life.

Of course, the downside is that you may either feel as if you're juggling a million matches, being pulled this way and that, or becoming emotionally indifferent to the people you date. It's important to remain focused on your love goal and not get caught up in the excitement of meeting as many new people as possible.

You know you're at risk for losing sight of your intention when you start forgetting the details of your dates. My client Joseph would ask me time and again to reiterate details of a particular match: "Where is she from again?" "Can you pull up her pictures one more time?" "Um, I forget if I had a good time with her . . . I think so?" He wasn't a player, but he *was* becoming a serial eDater. There's nothing wrong with this if fun alone is your goal! But I knew he wanted more. After I suggested that he slow down and focus on less quantity and more quality, he was able to take it all in, stay in the moment, and this time, remember every date's name.

Dating multiple people is necessary, whether you're seeking love or lust. So it's inevitable that new messages and dates will arrive in sync. Make sure you keep all of the logistics straight.

eDating Logistics

Scheduling is step number one to getting offline. When you're busy, like my client Monica, it can be tough to navigate, especially if more than one click mate is ready to meet offline. Monica often works late and prioritizes fitness and friendship, leaving most weeknights filled. Since meeting after work is preferred by most online daters, having lots of first meet-ups in a single week can get tricky for her to manage with an already-filled calendar. Her first instinct was to send her dates a link to her online calendar, allowing them to choose a free window of time that was convenient for them. It may have eliminated many back-and-forth emails, but productivity has a time and a place—and links to online calendars belong in the workplace, not the flirt place. Not surprisingly, guys would bail when they got a link to her Gcal, because a date should never feel like a scheduled meeting. I taught her that it's still possible to be efficient without becoming a Type A digi-dater. It's important to prioritize love in her life and set aside time each week to keep her dating life in motion.

On the other end of the spectrum, when Daniella got a message from a match about meeting, she'd put her entire life on hold until she heard back from him. She wouldn't make evening plans in advance with her girlfriends, on the off chance that he might choose that night for their date. Daniella needs to keep in mind that blowing off her friends all the time isn't a healthy way to begin a relationship. Putting life on hold until a date is planned is the digital equivalent of waiting by the phone.

Although both ladies' challenges are different, I taught them the same date-scheduling system.

1. Give someone two date options from your calendar. This shows that you can make time for dating in your life without seeming too available. From a scheduling perspective, it targets a few days in your calendar to leave open for dates so you can plan accordingly. Being specific should inspire your match to reply with a definite day and time, eliminating so much back-and-forth. If you're asking someone out on a date, this can be done in the same message. For example, "We should definitely grab that drink soon. How does Monday or Wednesday look for you?"

2. If you have multiple matches that are ready to meet up, ask one, and then wait twenty-four hours before asking out another. You'll probably have a response (and a date planned!) by then. Waiting a day between scheduling will limit conflicts and allow you to attempt to plan a date for the alternative day that your first match left open.

3. If you haven't heard back within twenty-four hours, go ahead and message your next date, but don't give specific times. That way, if the second match responds after your first match replies, you can give more specific suggestions. And if your first match still hasn't planned a meet-up by the time your other matches respond, feel free to book a date that you gave him or her. It's reasonable that schedules can shift in forty-eight hours.

4. If you have more than two dates to schedule at once, stay vague with your availability, and email them at the same time so you have room to plan. If it's more than you can handle in that week's calendar, keep the momentum going by responding that you want to meet up, but wait until they recommend dates to defer to another week.

Smitten or Spaced Out

While dating multiple people may seem like a juggling act, it can actually be more of an emotional marathon than a scheduling conflict. Emotionally separating yourself between dates is the most important part of flirting with multiple matches. To avoid feeling as if you're creating your very own WWE SmackDown: Dating Edition, keep the following points in mind:

> **Stay present and evaluate later.** When you're out with a match, focus on the person in front of you, and push thoughts of others to the wayside. As you begin to date more matches, this will become increasingly challenging, but if you can't stay in the moment, you'll never really give anyone a chance to make a lasting impression on you. Don't worry about your date next Wednesday, your work to-do list, or whether you'll get laid soon. Just focus on being part of the offline fun. You can compare how it went later.

> **Realize that dynamics are different.** It's inevitable that some relationships will click quickly while other sparks are a slow burn to fireworks. Friendships in your life are the same way: some people become immediate BFFs, but other relationships take time to build, and some will probably never make it into your inner circle. Some people make a great first impression but can fizzle, while others get better with time.

> **Pace yourself.** There is such a thing as overbooking. Three dates in one day will make your head spin (trust me, I speak from experience). And emotional exhaustion will set in if you meet up with a new person every night for weeks on end. While finding your click mate is important—and having fun should be a big part of that—if you overdo it, you'll get burned out before you get offline with your right click.

> **Don't ditch too soon.** After an uncharacteristically amazing date, it's not uncommon to feel that your other matches pale in comparison. But it's important not to give up on them just because a date with someone else went well. There's no way to tell if someone is really The One for you until you get to know each other better and determine if you gel over time.

〉 Know when to get serious. If you've been out more than five times with someone, you might want to slow down on dating other people. Even if you're not exclusive yet, it's time to focus your heart when it appears that things may be moving in that direction. But it's also not uncommon to feel like you need to dot your i's and cross your t's before committing to someone. If you are messaging multiple newbies simply to see what else is out there before you settle down, make sure you always put your heart first, whether that means canceling or continuing with new matches.

Double-Booking Do's

From time to time, dates might overlap. Don't freak—double-booking isn't preferred, but it's doable. If you're new to dating on the Web, only do this if they're both first meet-ups. Since these meetings are casual, it won't seem like flirtation overload.

But if you're a more seasoned digital dater, like April, you can venture into advanced date-scheduling territory. Circumstances caused a seemingly unavoidable situation for her. She had a first date booked already, and then a guy she'd been dating casually for a few weeks called. He was leaving town for a while, and the only opportunity she had to see him was on the same night as her first date. Concerned, she called me immediately, and after listening to my advice and taking a few deep breaths, she booked tickets for a late-night comedy show with her longer-term guy after early-evening first-meeting cocktails with the other one. And it was a success. Although she was initially nervous, she said afterward that it felt liberating to be in control. From a logistical standpoint, here are the tactics I relayed to April:

> **Be generous with timing.** Scheduling two dates in one day is not as simple as adding an appointment to your calendar. It's not predictable when you'll wrap up or as easy to bow out of your first date's company gracefully—especially if things are going well and you want to see him or her again! And of course, you'll need to switch gears mentally for your second date of the day, to remember what you've discussed so far, what you want to know more about, and, if it's a first meeting, a very crucial detail: his or her face! Consider how long the first date might take (including travel time), and leave a thirty to forty-five minute buffer. This will give you some extra time between dates to freshen-up and switch gears so you can focus more on your date's smile than on where the hands of your watch are pointing.

> **Vary locations.** Booking both dates at the same spot is a rookie mistake. While it may seem convenient for you, even scheduling in the neighborhood you've already been in is a major flirting hazard. Double-dating efficiency like this hardly ever goes according to plan. You never know if your date is going to decide to meet up with friends at the same locale after you leave or when the other match might arrive early. But don't make life too challenging for yourself; nearby neighborhoods are best. Being a few miles away means there's enough distance, but you're not running all over the place like a crazy person.

> **Save their numbers.** You should always have your matches' numbers before you get offline, in case life gets in the way. But it's more likely that you'll actually need their digits when you double-book, since timing can't be predicted down to the minute for your first date. Store their names, numbers, and avatars in your phone so you're prepared for anything.

> **Don't confuse your heart.** When double-booking, you should either be on the exact same date number with them (e.g., both first dates) or be on entirely opposite levels (e.g., a first date and a match you've been seeing for a few weeks). Being too close— but not the same—in date levels will only confuse you when your heart and mind compare situations, and you'll inevitably end up unjustly ruling one out.

> **Make sure you're not thrill-seeking.** During a message exchange, you should be able to get a feel for how excited your matches are. If you get the feeling that they're excited to meet you, there isn't any reason to double-book unless your schedule is too busy to see both on different days. And consider your intention. Are you doubling up for the thrill of it? This is common and not a bad thing—it's fun to date casually. But if you're looking for something serious, reconsider and reschedule.

If serial dating isn't your goal, there will come a time when you want to ax distractions.

It's completely natural for front-runners to develop when you date multiples. After working with Robbie for several months, I became worried that he was dismissing matches too quickly. Since I managed his online dating life, I was in control of his inbox and knew how many matches he'd met. He rarely went on a third date, and from our postdate chats, it seemed that he enjoyed the high of meeting someone new a little *too* much. This is common with thirty-something singles, but I knew that Robbie's intention was to find a long-term relationship. When Cameron crossed wires with him, I knew that she had staying power. I was surprised that his interest didn't wane after a few dates, but I knew I'd need to fight for it if I wanted him to stick with her. So I was sure to give lots of advice for continuing the momentum with Cameron.

In the past, Robbie had been shortsighted with relationships and would freak out when things started to get too deep emotionally. To keep him on solid ground with Cameron while he was dating other people online, I zeroed in on her during our coaching sessions. Having him recount his dates made him verbalize and own his feelings, bringing Cameron to the forefront of his heart. Then his actions and emotions could go deeper, sans panic attack. Soon enough, things with Cameron took off, and he stopped dating other people.

We'll address the specifics of logging off completely in chapter 13, but before you make any rash decisions to delete your other matches, make sure that your front-runner is worthy of your attention.

There are a few reasons you might want to put the rest of your online dating life on hold. In addition to craving a more serious relationship, at some point it might just seem weird and emotionally confusing to date multiples. Whether you're ready to get rid of the diversions in your love life or feel that you might be experiencing flirting overload, take a break from the matches you haven't met yet but are communicating with. This can be done without losing all of the traction you've developed with them so far. Allow your dating account to go inactive, so if you return a few weeks later, you can pick up with your other matches where you left off by feigning busy instead of later having to take back a major relationship announcement when you resurface in the world of online dating. If that shift does not offer enough of a break to keep your focus, you can also back off of your in-person matches. Staying in touch but not meeting up for dates will help put your conflicting emotions at ease but keep your matches interested until you've made more definite decisions about how you want to proceed.

As you scale back your flirting, keep in mind that after reading one profile and going on three dates, you've probably learned what interests you have in common with your front-runner, but you have yet to discover fully what values you share. So while taking down your profile one day is inevitable—and the goal if you're seeking a serious relationship—risking it all too soon can leave you more frustrated than being single with zero dating prospects. Until you're ready to have "the talk," remain open, and have fun. There's no rush!

CHAPTER 6

Digital Bodyguard

PROTECTING YOURSELF ONLINE AND OFF

Online safety is as important as looking both ways before you cross the street. But unfortunately, the Internet wasn't around when Mama filled you in on street smarts. If you're active online, you probably know your way around privacy policies, but keeping your digital dating life in the clear means much more than simply understanding the terms of service you're agreeing to when you join a dating site. In fact, staying safe in your eDating life is mostly achieved by being careful about what you reveal through your profile, in email exchanges, and even on the first date. How much do you really know about sunnyskies532 from a few message strings and one meet-up?

Many dating sites are taking preventative measures to protect your privacy. Most large dating sites are working in cooperation with the CA attorney general, specifically to reduce identity theft, financial scams, and sexual predation. They now check subscribers against the national sex-offender registries. Some sites go further by combing through profiles and removing ones that raise other red flags. And all sites are required to provide safety tips. It's important to review the specific tips for the sites you're on. Some scams are site-specific, and you'll want to educate yourself on anything common to the one you're using. Also, this resource will always be up-to-date.

But don't freak out: While this can sound scary, taking precautions when it comes to your online dating life doesn't differ from how you would handle meeting someone in the real world. It's freaky to think about, but the guy you met last night at the grocery store could just as easily be lying about his identity as the person you're messaging with. With that said, the best safety practices you learned growing up don't always translate digitally, so consider this your guide to avoiding cyber-creeps.

Don't Dish Dating Deets

Reveal the same level of information online that you might to a stranger chatting you up in a bar. Meeting online is essentially an introduction, so while you want to be specific in your profiles and emails, there is, of course, information that you should never give out until you've met and developed some level of trust. Here are the particulars you should always leave out of conversation until after your first date:

YOUR JOHN HANCOCK

Revealing your full name in your username, profile, or emails gives away your true identity. This is a major no-no for many reasons: now you are Googleable, can be found on social networks, and can be tracked in person. This is the biggest safety offense because until you get offline, you can never be 100-percent sure who's on the other side of the computer screen. So until you meet in person and there's trust in place, keep your full name under wraps, and only mention your first name to be friendly.

USERNAME OVERLAP

Pick a username that you haven't used anywhere else in your life. If you use your AIM screen name, your Facebook username, or anything else associated with your personal identity, matches can Google it and easily find out more information on you. Usernames not only track back to you, but they often also lead to your friends' social media pages and stats. Back in the day, online daters on paid sites used their go-to usernames on purpose so matches could find them off the site and communicate without having to shell out the dough for a full subscription. But these days, there are plenty of free sites to choose from. If your budget doesn't allow for a subscription to a dating site, don't compromise your safety; register for a free one.

DISCLOSING DIGITS

Give out your phone number only once you've emailed a few times and feel comfortable. And when you do send your digits, the best virtual safety device is to register for a Google Voice number. This allows you to chat with your match without someone being able to trace the number to your personal information. And if you don't feel a connection, you can easily block the person's number after you meet. (Just be sure to download the Google Voice app so you have full functionality, such as text-messaging from that number, too.)

If you're still not comfortable giving out a number when your date-to-be asks, just get his or her digits instead. You can either dial worry-free from the Google Voice app or hit *67 before dialing through your normal line so your number comes up as private. Luckily for you, both services are freebies.

REGULAR REMOVAL

While I encourage you to be specific in your profile, don't mention places you go to so often that a hostess, waiter, or bartender knows your name. If you're at a particular locale on a weekly basis, banish it from your profile. Not only would it be awkward to run into your match at your favorite restaurant, but it's also a security breach. So unless he or she lives in your neighborhood, internal alarms should sound if you happen to run into each other.

YOUR ADDRESS

Your home and work addresses should always be kept under wraps. If you're an urban dweller, it's OK to mention the general neighborhood you live in, but steer clear of being block-specific and too specific about nearby landmarks, such as parks. It's OK to discuss these places as favorites of yours; just don't mention their proximity to your home. The same goes for vacation homes, friends' residences, and family homes; giving too much information about any of these allows someone to trace you.

COMPANY SPECIFICS

As I mentioned in chapter 3, you should absolutely mention what your day-to-day consists of. So go ahead and describe your favorite part of your job, but steer clear of anything too specific. Listing your title is fine, as long as it isn't unique to your company. Otherwise, it will be easy to find you on LinkedIn or Facebook if you list your exact job description there, too.

My client Marisol is a forty-five-year-old partner at a presti-gious consulting firm. Even though it's an enormous company, there are very few people who have her same title. And when it's paired with her first name, you can locate her on the Internet. Keep your career close, but your company's name closer.

Entrepreneurs are particularly guilty here. It's understand-able to want to brag about your accomplishments; you're prob-ably emotionally attached to this part of your life. But skip the name-dropping. It's not only unsafe, but you may attract the wrong kinds of matches—particularly if your company's $15 million in Series B funding was just announced on CNBC.

Along the same lines, being involved in a charity, a founda-tion, or a board is impressive and should definitely make its way into your profile. But before shouting out the organization's name, check its website to make sure your name and bio aren't listed on the site. You can always keep things vague by focusing on the nature of the cause rather than the organization.

LINK LOVE

Blog posts you've written, videos you appear in, social media accounts you're active on, and articles you've been quoted in should be left out entirely. Any Web link about you will inevi-tably lead to more links and information about who you are, opening up the Pandora's box of your cyber-past and your offline life. Additionally, from a self-marketing perspective, you're sending your matches *away* from the site where they can communicate with you, which will ultimately mean a lower click-through to your inbox.

Links can also be overwhelming for readers. My client Jody once wrote a blog post about her perfect man—and linked to it in her profile. As an author and a famous Internet personality, she's used to promoting her work on the Web. But besides potentially breaching her own safety online, the link was also information overload for her matches. It made prospective dates feel as if they needed to tick off every single box of perfection before they could send her a message, which possibly made her come off as excessively picky. And in addition to reading her profile, they now also had a seven-hundred-word blog post to read, which meant that they had to spend more time figuring out whether to communicate with her. Needless to say, removing all of the .coms was my first edit to her profile.

THINK BEFORE YOU TWEET

Your social media privacy settings are important, too. In the age of oversharing, knowing what your match can have access to will help you decide how to proceed. Assume that a match can find any of your social media profiles. Unless your Twitter account is private, anyone can read your updates. So if you tweet that you're out on a date, other matches might read it. And if you toggle your Foursquare updates, anywhere you check in is available to the public.

Also, be particularly cautious of comments in the cloud from followers and friends that can be misconstrued as flirtatious or of uploading photos of you and someone of the same sex as your match. If someone sends you a friend request on Facebook and finds a wall riddled with red flags, you may find your dating calendar dwindling.

YOUR EMAIL ADDRESSES

If people have your personal or work email address, they can find anything digitally tethered to it: your LinkedIn profile, the

MySpace account you haven't used in years but never officially deleted, your membership to an alumni association, and so on.

Janice is a great gal but a search-engine addict. When I met her, she filled me in on her online prowess—how she'd email guys and then ask for an email address so she could take to the Google streets. With one match, she found out not only his company and his last name but also more personal matters such as the listing of the sale of his home, his ex-wife's name, and his child's dean's-list announcement. Suddenly, this man's entire world was at her fingertips, including information that wasn't even accurate.

Communicate through the site rather than through personal-email inboxes. Not only is it a breach of safety, but it's not as convenient. You want to get offline seamlessly with matches, not make them jump through cyber-hoops to stay connected to you. Treat your email address like gold. Go on a few dates, and make sure you really click with your match before revealing your addy.

Occasionally, your matches will ask to move conversation to email territory for a valid reason; maybe their subscriptions are ending or they feel more comfortable on their personal email. But be aware that this can be a major red flag for fraud. Think about it: scammers know that fraudulent behavior can be detected by the dating site police. To avoid being caught, they'll opt to conduct their sneaky third-degree in a more private environment. Proceed with caution.

In the rare instance when you need to communicate off the site with someone, give him or her an email that isn't affiliated with your personal life. Create a new Gmail, Yahoo!, or AOL account, and don't use your complete last name when you register. This will permit you to communicate safely without revealing any new information to your match—until you meet for a fabulous first date.

Scam Jam, Thank You, Ma'am

If people recommend emailing off the site, it's possible that they could be fakes, communicating to scam you instead of woo you. Give your entire email string a second read to make sure you know where their intentions lie and ask yourself the following questions with disingenuous behavior in mind.

1. How many emails have you exchanged? In most cases, scammers will want to get off the site immediately. Dropping their email addresses in their first message to you is a huge indication that their intentions aren't genuine. Often their email addresses are accompanied by requests to use an instant messenger service, too. Look for email addresses that do not end with ".com." Scammers are typically in other countries, so they can't be as easily traced. Or they'll use email providers that aren't as picky about linking domains to another country.

2. Do they use flowery language? Fraudulent members often use romantic language in their messages. If you feel as if someone's getting awfully intimate in the first few messages (like, way more than what you're comfortable with or what you'd typically expect), that's a tip-off that things may not be on the up-and-up. Normal matches don't bear their soul right away. For example, scammers might mention how many children they want to have, share sob stories about how they lost their first spouses, or be all about candlelight and walks on the beach. Words such as "destiny" or "fate" are also tip-offs that they might not be genuine.

3. Is the digital conversation confusing? In most cases, the first few emails from fraudulent users are copy-and-paste templates. If they ignore questions you ask or cover topics you've already discussed, it's likely that all is not right. It's often easy to write these inaccuracies off as oversights, but pay close attention when you review your message strings. Are these people genuinely missing your questions and shifting back to material that's previously been covered, or are they responding with template emails that make no sense?

4. Does their grammar lead you to believe that English isn't their first language? As I mentioned, deceitful members are often located abroad. Perhaps it's just the match's style of writing but often the nationalities in their photos, their education levels, and their grammatical errors don't quite jibe. If your match is a doctor who doesn't list another country as his birthplace, you can be pretty sure that he wouldn't write, "Thanks alot for taking your time to write me I really apprecient , im new to this online dating. you actually the first person im having free and fair commincaition." Alternately, some scammers emails are *too* well-written and usually come off overeducated even to a Harvard grad. Sometimes matches like this will say that they are local but are currently working in another country—some will even pose as soldiers stationed in war zones for the sympathy factor!

5. Do their profiles suddenly disappear? As I mentioned, dating sites are constantly trying to protect you from fraudulent members. When they detect behavior that seems a little off, they quickly remove users that raise red flags from their sites. If matches you're communicating with suddenly do a disappearing act without mentioning that they were taking their profiles down, it could mean that they were removed by site administration.

6. Do they look too good to be true? Scammers typically impersonate matches who are most likely to be perceived by you as out of your league. That way, you feel like they're too perfect to pass over and are more forgiving of all these issues. As a woman who has a thing for guys with light eyes and dark hair, I can tell you that even digitally, a guy who makes me weak in the knees challenges my better judgment. If you think you've fallen in love merely with a digital persona, take his or her pictures out of the equation and look at the facts. The words are all right there in front of you—does everything add up?

7. Do they have emergencies that require borrowing money? Scammers ultimately want you to pay up, something that happens after you move to a personal email address. If you felt that they passed all of the above tests but you suddenly get a frantic email about a vacation gone bad, stop right there. Do not pass Go. Do not shell out two hundred dollars—although typically, they'll ask for much more. Their story might go like this: She was vacationing in another country and had her wallet stolen, and the Consulate won't help since her passport was also swiped by the pickpocket. Or he'll pose as a soldier stationed abroad near a war zone and ask for money to cover a flight home to visit you. Never ever give a match money, your credit card, your bank information, or your Social Security Number. Unless you're in a committed relationship, have gone on dates, and slept over at each other's house—many times— you shouldn't ever let someone "borrow" money. If withholding money is emotionally challenging for you, just imagine how you'll feel when they vanish after you deposit thousands of dollars into their bank account. When you decline their request via email, and they don't respond—or they do respond and bash you—remember that it's only because they're upset that they wasted time and energy on messages to you without receiving their payday.

8. Do they dodge dates? You'll never meet a scammer in person. Usually they aren't even local, but they will get your hopes up and make plans over and over again. This will keep you emotionally involved and make your heart yearn for more; making it more likely you'll open your wallet to them. When they dodge dates, they will always have a good reason for the cancellation—like being hospitalized—that you won't be able to argue with. But let's get one thing straight—getting offline with your matches is the most important part of dating online. If they continually cancel on you, it's time to move on. They might have good reasons to dodge your dates, but the three-strike rule applies here: under no circumstances should you continue communicating with someone who cancels on you that often. In fact, they should consider themselves lucky if you don't remove them from your prospects after *one* cancellation. I know this all too well, because back in my early days of online dating, I met a date dodger in an AOL chat room (I told you I've been dating digitally for a while!). Since there was no information for situations like this, I was unsure how to handle it. Take it from me, cutting off communication sooner rather than later will save you heartache.

Sites like RomanceScam.org house a scammer database that you can check if you think you've been duped. Their technical team will help you determine the location an email was sent from (via IP address) and the authenticity of documents they may have sent to try and sway you (like Visas).

It's important to report scammy members to the site so they can't harm others. There's usually a button that allows you to do this easily. But most safety breaches won't be serious. You should be aware of the worst-case scenarios, but the average online dater typically encounters only people who are authentically interested in you but want to do a Google search before meeting to check you out further.

Being aware of what the Internet has on you is half the battle. When information in your profile is combined with your first name, it will often result in your digital identity. This isn't a big cause for concern; very few matches will make it their goal to comb your profile for multiple words to pair with your name and city so they can find you online, but either way, you should be aware of the results. Open a fresh Web page, and do your own search to make sure that you're in the clear. For example, type in your first name and either the career description from your profile or any organizations you're affiliated with (like your university or gym). If nothing pops up on the first two pages, add your profile city or town to see if anything comes up that way.

Armed with this information, you can decide whether it's worth it to edit your profiles further to ensure your virtual protection. If your name is particularly rare, like Zahara, you'll be even more susceptible to search engines. In this case, think about giving matches a nickname for yourself. A nickname is even more important on algorithm-based sites, which require you to take your real name public versus creating a username.

Just make sure that it's an attractive one. Although your family might call you Zippy, that doesn't make for the most feminine first impression. If you only have nicknames that you'd need to explain in order to make them endearing, come up with something else, or use your initial only (such as Z).

Keep Offline and Online Realities Consistent

Once you and your matches have been on a few dates, they'll inevitably know your full name. Search engines are essentially a portal to your past, so make sure you're ready to give people access to this information when you fill them in on your full name. You want to make sure there's consistency between what they've learned about you so far and your Google results. If the only results are your Facebook page and LinkedIn profile, there shouldn't be any cause for concern. But if your wedding announcement to your ex-wife is on the first Google search page, you might want to think about doing some digital damage control.

This was the case for Sarah. A bisexual single, she dated both men and women but fell for a lucky lady in college. They had a wonderful marriage but eventually divorced amicably. After a few years, she decided to date men again. The only snafu was that when you entered her name into a search engine, the very first result was the *New York Times* announcement of her wedding to Melissa. This is obviously an extreme case, but had she not known that the article existed, she would have been caught totally off-guard if a match asked about it point-blank on a date.

The same can happen with any morsel of information, whether it's actually you or not, such as the felony someone with your same age and name committed. You can always try reaching out to whoever published the piece and attempt to have it removed from the site. But if it's a large news source or a government-regulated page, it will be challenging. Sarah reached out to the *Times* but was told that nothing could be done about her wedding anouncement. In cases like this, Google and Bing both recommend that you publish more positive information about yourself, like blog posts mentioning your name, to try to outrank the piece you'd prefer that others don't see.

If You're Uncomfortable, Deflect

Inevitably, on your way to becoming an online dating success story, conversations will come up that steer into territory you'd rather not enter so soon. This isn't usually intentional; most matches are asking because they're genuinely interested in getting to know you. But you should still guard your safety.

If a topic comes up that is a safety breach, there's no need to get defensive the first time around. Just deflect the question. One such email string happened with one of my clients:

> From: typedwriter
> Sent: October 23 12:19 PM
> To: uprightbeats
> Subject: RE: One Note Above
> Hey Michelle,
> Great that your last concert went well and glad your parents were able to make the trip to see you play. Where in the city do you live? I'm on 72nd and Broadway.
> It would be great to meet in person. Let me know where you are, and we can meet near you.
> Alec

Hcy Alec,
I love 72nd street! Aroma Espresso Bar is one of my favorite coffee shops in the whole city. The outdoor space is gorgeous this time of year. Let's meet there—I haven't been in a while. Does Sunday work for you?
Michelle

As you can see, Michelle made the transition off the private topic seamlessly and deflected the question without making it awkward. The best way to deflect while keeping the energy of the message moving forward is to expand on the topic and keep to the same level of excitement that the match projected.

Be Your Own P.I.

Get in the digital know about your date's background; it's important for you to stay informed, too. But unless something seems suspicious, you should wait to take any of the measures below until you've met offline. Just as your background can be misconstrued when someone who doesn't know you well views it, you can just as easily misread a match's past. Allow your date to make his or her own first impression rather than letting Google take the reins.

After your first date, here are recommended ways of checking up on your click mate to make sure your heart is in safe hands—from the least obtrusive to the most in-depth:

> **Use search engines.** Let's face it, the Internet is smart. Today everyone leaves a virtual bookmark somewhere on the Web. Pri-

oritize open social networks for viewing their uninhibited, real-time worlds. Next, browse legal announcements. Finally, read articles by them (or about them) and other miscellaneous digital traces that may be left behind. If your cyber-scouring doesn't result in at least three hits for your match, you're either doing something wrong or you should think twice before continuing. Lack of digital information could mean that a person has something to hide.

> **Get connected.** Social platforms are a great way to find out more about someone without being too intrusive. See if your circles and networks overlap; mutual friends, colleagues, or acquaintances are a good place to start. Viewing more information online about the connections might lead you to additional information. And you can always drop a hint to your common pal (if you're close with the person) to find out what their relationship is like. Social recon is sometimes the most valuable because it will tell you things that Web searches can't, like how someone is perceived by others.

> **Do a background check.** While this is a more invasive approach, it's definitely something you should consider if you're interested in your match but have a weird feeling that all is not right. If there's one thing I've learned from many years of online dating, it's that you need to trust your gut. There are background check services that will do a quick look for you using their software or a more personalized option that will use former police officers to uncover details about your date. Robert Buchholz, the cofounder of MyMatchChecker.com, a background-check company that specifically helps online daters, advises you to look first for vio-

lent offenses and sexually deviant behavior when receiving a report on a match. Felony charges are the most serious. However, if someone has an extended history of driving violations, that could be a sign of his or her level of maturity.

Weaving an Offline Safety Web

It's not all about what happens digitally. While your relationship may start online, it's important to remain cautious for at least the first few dates as you develop a rapport with each other. Here are safety guidelines to follow when you meet-up:

⟩ **Meet in public.** The first time you meet a match, others should be around. The safest options are coffee shops, bars, or other establishments where there are bound to be a good number of people. Some public places are less preferable than others, though. Parks, lakes, or places where private or semi-private nooks and crannies exist are better for the second part of the date, once you feel more comfortable, or for a second date.

⟩ **Get there on your own.** Whether you drive, take a taxi, or use public transit, make sure you arrive at the date on your own. The most important thing is that you have the ability to leave whenever you choose. If your date ends up being a dud, you want to make sure you're not tied to someone else's schedule and can leave when you like.

⟩ **Have a backup.** Always give yourself an out in case things get tricky. Whether you want to leave because you're bored or sketched out, mentioning that you have dinner plans or an early morning the next day will suffice. But if your date won't budge and needs more convincing, there are actually apps for that. One of my favorites-of-the-moment is eHarmony's Bad Date Rescue app, which gives multiple solutions for getting out of a day or a night out if your date is being particularly insistent that you continue. Take a trip to the bathroom, and schedule a faux "emergency" phone call or a calendar appointment you "forgot." Five minutes later, you'll have digital proof that it's time to go.

〉 **Watch your drink.** Keep an eye on your cocktail or coffee. While it may seem paranoid to keep it in your possession all the time, the roofie risk is real on any date, regardless of where you met. That said, it will most certainly seem comical and paranoid to your date if you are seated at a table and go to the bathroom with your vodka soda in tow. Either try finishing your drink before nature calls, or refrain from sips after you return.

〉 **Walking home.** If you live in an urban area and your date knows you're in your neighborhood, he or she might insist on walking you home. Politely decline, to avoid revealing your address. But on the off chance that he or she insists, preselect a doorman building near your own residence. Allow your date to walk you there, and keep the fact that it's not your building hidden. Closing the night with a phrase like, "This is where I'll leave you" is open-ended enough that if the relationship continues, you can reveal your safety savvy without embarrassment.

> **Wait to be alone together.** Wait until at least the second date to be alone in either of your homes. If you're seeking a serious relationship, getting a nightcap or venturing into bedroom behavior on a first date isn't advised, anyway. But if you're looking for a more casual relationship and want to move things along physically, go to his or her place. That way, you can still leave on your own terms, and your address is kept under wraps. And if your date is not OK with that, wait until date two to ask him or her back to your place, when you've had more time to get to know each other.

> eFlirt Byte: According to OkCupid's study of online dating lies, singles fib mostly through insignificant details like height (most increase by two inches) and income (people exaggerate by 20 percent).

It can be unnerving to wonder constantly if your dates are telling the truth about who they are. But since most singles only tell white lies in their profiles, don't worry every minute that your soon-to-be date is an ax murderer or hiding an enormous secret; it's more likely that there are much less significant inaccuracies in the profiles you'll view.

There is also such a thing as being *too* safe. When your safety precautions dramatically limit your dating options, you're probably keeping your cards too close. You can absolutely let someone know what your personality is like without feeling like you're handing over your Social Security Number. This shouldn't be hard, since your profile is a first impression, not a revelation of deep, dark secrets.

Limit your profile and eCommunication to what you feel comfortable with, but don't limit your descriptions so much that you sound nondescript. If you keep things too general, you could appear like a scammer yourself! But most important, you never want to come across as guarded or defensive; instead, let your persona reveal that you're open to the possibility of finding your right click.

CHAPTER 7

Search Strategy

NAVIGATING THROUGH MATCHES

When you're online, it becomes challenging not to judge an eBook by its cover, because, well, all you *have* is the cover. A first impression. A few photos. A profile.

As you scroll through the thumbnails of faces, it's nearly impossible not to start comparing matches against one another. If you're not careful, you'll soon find yourself only clicking on the hottest members of the site and dismissing them one by one, because they don't measure up to the ePrince or ePrincess you've dreamt up. It's easy to have unrealistic expectations online that you wouldn't necessarily have in real life, simply because there are so many options. So how can you keep an open mind? First, let's look at the four main ways you're categorizing your matches—even if you don't notice it.

Learning Your ABCs . . . and Ds

When viewing a profile, you think either (A) definitely yes, (B) OK, (C) maybe, or (D) no way. But simplicity can be deceiving. Here's what these categories translate into:

> **A list.** Someone on your A list is ideal. He or she is incredibly attractive and seems to have every single quality you're looking for.

> **B list.** Potential mates on this list have most of the traits you're looking for in a date but are (or seem to be) missing a few things. They're OK but not your top choices.

> **C list.** The matches on this list leave you undecided. Perhaps they're funny but not so cute. Or they're good-looking, but wit is lacking. Some qualities are great, and some aren't, so you're torn.

> **D list.** There's nothing about these profiles that strikes you as attractive, and you can often make this determination rather quickly.

Now, let me give you a reality check. People are dynamic, with tons of nuances and fluctuations that don't translate when viewing them on a screen. There's much more to an individual than *appearances* in a profile.

An A-list match who seems amazing on paper may be underwhelming when you meet in person and are exposed to the complete package. The other truth about A-listers is that someone who projects virtual perfection normally has an overflowing inbox, making him or her less likely to respond to you. So focusing all of your efforts on the top echelon of online daters can prove disappointing for many reasons. On the flip side, while it's easy to dismiss those on your B and C lists, your D list should automatically be rejected.

Maybes online are entirely different from the maybes you meet in person.

Bs and Cs have the most hidden potential—much more than a five-hundred-word-count profile and a few pictures give them credit for. There's always a chance that they can impress you beyond the broadband.

When my client Jack set up a date with Rosemary, he was *not* excited. I tried to pump up his energy, but he was expecting the night to be a failure. Her photos were only OK, and her profile was sparse. But when she showed up, he nearly fell off his chair—she was gorgeous, leggy, *and* she made him laugh. Automatic catapult from a C to an A!

In real life, thinking "maybe" during the dating process is a red flag; if you say it about a partner, perhaps you should reconsider your pending relationship. But those judgments are educated, based on actions and discussion face-to-face. There are many more barriers online that can keep people's best self from shining through. Their profiles only reveal what they *think* they should write to say hello to the masses, not a conversation they would have if they were meeting you one-on-one. And if their photos leave something to be desired, perhaps they don't have good, recent ones to upload.

Truly putting yourself out there involves communicating with those on your A, B, and C lists so you don't risk passing over The One.

Dating Management To-Dos

You can't manage your online dating life without first strategizing your plan of action; otherwise, it's unclear *what* you're managing and how you'll define your success. Whether you're a digital dating vet or not, developing an online dating strategy— and reviewing it once a month—will help keep you on track.

> **Log-in routine.** There's a time and a place for everything, including online dating. Whether checking your flirting inbox comes before or after you devour the *Wall Street Journal* online, logging in should be a part of your daily Internet routine. Giving yourself a small, manageable goal to achieve each day will help keep your dating life moving forward. Quantifying your goal in either time or emails is the best approach. Eli Finkel, professor of psychology at Northwestern and lead author of a study on online dating, suggests that you stay aware of the amount of profiles you've viewed in one sitting and create a set time in which to browse them. So either commit thirty minutes a day to online dating or send three new messages per sitting until you have a full flirting agenda.

> **Inbox cleanup.** If you're not interested in a match, there's no reason to have his or her messages lingering in your account. Delete them, and leave more room for the ones who have offline potential. Just be sure not to throw a match into the trash too soon; if you're making a heat-of-the-moment decision because someone canceled a date, you might feel renewed interest in that person, and you'll want to have your past email string so you're armed with information you can refer back to.

> **Leverage features.** Make sure that you're intimately involved with your dating site. Knowing the ins and outs of how it functions and all of the features that are available will keep you effi-

cient. For example, most sites allow you to hide matches you're not interested in. Taking the time to hide people who aren't your speed while you search—and, of course, those matches who you dated but just weren't The One—will keep your options streamlined.

>> Profile tweaks. In a browse-based flirting world, you want to make sure that you stay at the top of your matches' search results, giving you a steady stream of incoming cuties. The easiest way to keep a fresh face is to update your profile photos—on most sites, adding a new picture will automatically send you to the top of people's search results. Choose two pics more than you need for your profile, and keep alternating between the two—delete one and upload another each week. Another option is to make minor edits to the text of your profile. For example, on Match.com, you can update the For Fun section with activities from the past weekend. Doing this any time of the week should optimize your ranking, but updating on high-traffic days is best.

eFlirt Byte: Most sites agree
that Sunday is one of the most active
days for eFlirting.

Beyond the day-in-and-day-out of your attraction actions, your strategy should shift depending on the type of site you're on. As I mentioned in chapter 2, there are sites that allow you to search and others that deliver matches to you based on algorithms.

Checklist for Searching

For search-based sites, follow these rules for narrowing down your lists:

> **Create broad filters.** On the search page, begin by browsing based on the broadest range of characteristics you're looking for. This could include a ten-year age span, a twenty-mile radius from your residence, a ten-inch height range, and so on. Beginning your journey by viewing a larger group of possible matches that will make your heart pitter-patter will encourage you to keep an open mind moving forward.

> **Save your search criteria.** Knowing what you've searched for in the past will allow you to be efficient in the future. When the functionality of the site allows, save the particulars you've combed through so far. This way, you can search all of the page results of one group of singles completely before moving on to the next, making your right click easier to spot.

> **Don't count.** Keeping track of every single message you send and receive will cause unnecessary heartache. You're looking for a match, not trying to reach the high score on a video game! It's OK to be aware of how you're doing, but it can throw you off your game if you analyze too in-depth all the time. Focus on finding your click mate instead of gaming the system.

> **Alter your criteria.** Editing the specifics of your filters every week or two will allow you to see fresh faces. Changing your age range by one year, looking within a new zip code, or adding an inch to your height preferences will show you new matches with potential. Once you've searched broadly, feel free to narrow

your preferences every once in a while and maybe even search outside your comfort zone.

> **Don't fall in virtual love.** Don't get too caught up with a single profile. Love at first click can't truly be experienced until the relationship goes live. My clients who fall in eLust before meeting are always disappointed. And sometimes over-enthusiasm reads on-screen, discouraging your match from even replying. Wait until you're in person before allowing yourself to get emotionally involved.

> **Log in frequently.** Doing this makes your profile more approachable. Having been online recently means you're more likely to be an active member who will receive their digital messages quickly. On some sites, members have the ability to search by those who are "online now" or by users who have logged in recently. So even when you're having a busy week and can't meet your dating goals, make sure to log in every few days to get the eDating VIP treatment. When you're searching, take note of your matches' last log-ins. Ideally, you want to message members who have been on the site at least three days prior—anything longer, and it's possible they've had their last log *off*.

> **Review those newbies.** Most sites will tell you who their newest members are. If you start feeling like you're seeing the same matches over and over, checking out new members will freshen up your approach to your dating life.

> **Check out who is checkin' you out.** On most search-based sites, you can see who has viewed your profile. This is often an overlooked feature. After all, if someone views your profile and

likes you, wouldn't he or she send a message? But if you make the first move, singles are often just as likely to respond. If they were on the verge of emailing but ultimately decided not to, a note from you could sway them to say hello back. So if someone has clicked on you but didn't shoot you a message, go ahead and be the first to reach out. Just don't mention that you saw their view—it can come off creepy.

Picking Your Preferences

On algorithm-centric sites, your dates are curated for you, so your focus should shift to tailoring your tastes. Don't worry, these sites will still throw you a curve ball from time to time to make sure you're looking beyond your comfort zone. But the more specific you are, while remaining open-minded, the more likely you'll frequently get matches that resonate with you. Here are the particulars for making the most of those algorithms:

> **Create narrow filters.** On algorithm sites, your match selection is limited; they curate a specific number for you per day. So rather than creating wide filters as you would on search-based sites to see everyone under a broad set of criteria, you want to go narrow to maximize the limited number of results you receive. Do this by being honest with yourself about whom you're looking for in your settings. Your filters are private, so you won't have to worry about other matches judging you based on your narrow criteria. If you consider yourself spiritually open-minded but would really prefer to date within your religion, start by checking only your faith off the list so those matches are prioritized. You can add more checkmarks to the list of religions later on, once the site has sent you most of its same-faith singles.

› Get specific with importance. For each trait, the site will usually ask how important it is to you. If you indicate that it's not important, the site will take more liberties with whom you're matched with. For example, if you select the body types you're attracted to and then indicate that you don't really care, the site might match you with types outside those you checked off. If you're picky about a particular set of criteria, tick only the types you're open to, and note that it's extremely important so that the algorithm stays within your preferences.

› Watch for trends. When you start seeing patterns of matches you're not attracted to, it's time to tweak your filters. Without feedback from time to time, the algorithm won't be able to get it just right. For example, perhaps your settings say that you have a master's degree but that a similar level of education isn't important to you. If you notice that you continue to get sent matches who have only done "some college" and you'd really prefer someone with at least a bachelor's, it's time to log on and bump up the level of importance you're placing on education.

› Edit filters once a month. Each month, revisit your filters to check in with where you stand on what you're indicating as preferences. Trust me, your tastes will change based on your dating experiences, so setting it up once and leaving it be won't get you the best results online or offline. And if you notice that the rate of matches you receive each day is slowing down, that's a sign that the site is struggling to fit all of your criteria. Open up some of your preferences, and your inbox will fill up with flirtables.

As a true Southern gent, my client David wanted to keep an open mind, so his filters were far-reaching: one hundred twenty miles from his zip code, a fifteen-year age range, and any ethnicity, income range, lifestyle preferences, religion, and so on. While he got many matches, his eFlirting life remained stagnant. Ladies from other states weren't into meeting, and his inbox remained silent. He was open-minded—to a fault—because his matches didn't always see things the same way. Once we changed his partner preferences to be more focused (and local), his dating life took off.

Just make sure that you're not making snap judgments when you eliminate someone from your screen. If your match's photo is kind of OK but you're not inspired to send an email, don't immediately hit Delete. If the person updates his or her pics later on, you might have a change of heart.

And while you've been schooled in best profile practices, that doesn't mean every match you come across will be in the-know. If you like someone, be forgiving of a few generic lines here and there or an online dating cliché or two.

Do you prefer quantity or quality of matches? Deciding which is your priority means you're more likely to find digital dating happiness. If you'd prefer quantity of dates, keep your options open, and strategize to reach more people. But if you prefer quality and are seeking someone special, focus on matches of substance.

While there will be rare instances when the first person you message turns into The One, online dating is typically a journey and, like anything in life, worth waiting for. It takes persistence, thought, and a little bit of time. But don't get so caught up in the details that you forget to put fun on your agenda.

Red-Flag Revolution

EMPOWERING DIGITAL SELECTION

Online dating isn't entirely about what *you* put out online; having an awesome experience also means playing defense. Knowing how to read between the lines of the profiles you encounter will help you determine who's worth an email and a date . . . and which matches are better left alone. This is all especially true if you're looking for a lifetime love. Serious seeking singles typically want to avoid the riffraff more than those who are going casual for now in their dating life. But, as usual, the digital universe and the offline world aren't always in sync.

Online red flags are not necessarily offline deal breakers.
In real life, we trust our guts to tell us if something isn't right. But when you remove the face-to-face element, your instincts might be a little off. Naturally, you have fewer life lessons to draw from to pick up on warning signs when dealing with someone screen-to-screen.

But being too exclusive might mean missing out on Mr. or Ms. Almost Right on virtual paper, who could transition into

The One after you meet beyond the broadband. So keep these red flags in mind, while *still* exploring your A, B, and C lists.

In the online dating process, red flags can crop up in a number of places—a match's profile, your email communications, or offline. Let's take a look at each.

Profiles

Knowing how to read a profile is crucial to using the hours you log online effectively. Certain nuances will help you determine which matches to prioritize. Let's break profiles down section by section.

PHOTOS

You can learn a lot about people when you view their pics. Not only can you determine whether you find them attractive at first glance, but you can also make below-the-surface judgments. If they're posing with others, take a peek at their friends; their appearance might reveal more than you think about the company they keep and the types of social activities they frequent. What people wear reveals their style and the level of care they take with themselves. And activities and action shots reveal their lifestyles, like an affinity for fitness if they're crossing a marathon finish line.

Having no photos speaks louder than any words you could type. But this isn't uncommon, particularly for forty-plus singles. People are often quick to jump to conclusions about picture-less members, but think twice before you do. If they lack photos *and* their profile is generic, skip to the next ASAP. But if they mention a good reason for lacking photos and have well-put-together profiles, it might be worth emailing them. My client

Diane was a vice president at a publicly traded financial firm, and her employment contract included a clause that banned her from posting photos on any dating site. So while lacking a photo can certainly be a red flag, there are exceptions. Be on the safe side, though; it's good practice to keep yourself on the defensive while you communicate. Lacking photos could also mean someone's hiding something . . . like a tan line on his or her left ring finger.

While posting a profile with no photos can be confusing, having only one photo is even more baffling. If the one image is from far, far away and you can barely make the person's features out, he or she doesn't want to be seen clearly or be easily identified. And if the pic is a close-up of the person's face, there might be a reason for not revealing a full bod; perhaps the listed body type and actual size in person don't match up.

Pixilated and grainy photos typically mean that they're outdated, and there's usually a correlation between old photos and listing an inaccurate age.

CONTENT

A lot can be determined about people by how they project themselves on paper. Pay close attention to the way they describe themselves and the tone used. As a rule of thumb, the more a person distances him or herself from what they type, the more likely it is that the eDater is lying.

eFlirt Byte: Psychologists at the University of Wisconsin-Madison found that people who use fewer first-person pronouns (like "I") and negative words (like "not" and "never") are more likely to be lying.

Length can also be an indicator of digital fibbing. If your matches don't write much about themselves, it could mean they're hiding something. And a sparse profile may mean that someone is taking a casual approach to dating and isn't looking for anything long-term. One way to determine intent is to send a content-rich email and see if he or she responds in kind. If so, then the match is probably into you.

YOU

How people write about their ideal match is also an intention indicator. Take note not only of how they talk about themselves but also their mentions of a match. Ultimatums are common but often translate into being closed-minded and restrictive when meeting new people. If their descriptions of "you" are equal in length to or longer than their own descriptions of themselves, it's a red flag that their laundry lists are far too long and unrealistic.

On the opposite end of the spectrum, it's not a good sign if this section is absent, either. Singles who skip this step completely might not have a clear idea of whom they'd like to meet or might only be in it for fun. If you're looking for a fling, this shouldn't be an issue. But for long-term love, you'll want to know that your match has standards and has given thought to what he or she prioritizes in a mate. Plus, knowing what one wants is usually a sign of maturity.

In the digital domain, some phrases should raise an eyebrow.
Now that you know the places you should be paying attention to in a profile, let's break down particular phrases that are often loaded with meaning—and not in a good way. Table 2 shows some common lines that you'll see and what they might *really* mean.

Table 2. Decoding Date Speak

PHRASE	MEANING
"It's OK if we're friends first"	Playing the friendship card before they've even met you is a telltale sign that they may not be ready to commit.
"Don't worry, I'll lie and say we met in real life"	They're not comfortable with online dating, and it might be a challenge to get them offline at all. And if they're willing to make up a story about how you met, they might not be as honest as you'd hope.
"I hate drama"	If drama is on your match's mind, it's likely that there is still some lingering in his or her own life. And even if not, it could mean that the match has been burned by drama in the past, which is now part of his or her own baggage.
"Email me"	If a match has to request an email from you, confidence is typically lacking.
"I'm not sure exactly how to describe myself"	While some people who say this are humble, it's more likely that they're lacking self-confidence, and this can spill over into other parts of their lives.
"Out of the gutter"	If a match mentions getting minds out of the gutter, it was probably always there to begin with. Well-placed jokes are the exceptions to this rule.
"I'm just trying this out"	This shows lack of commitment. They're uncomfortable with online dating and often not very serious about meeting someone.
"My ideal match would be just like [celebrity]"	Beware the name-droppers. Those who discuss celebs in their profiles usually value looks above all else, since it's rare that they've met a superstar personally. This can also signal unrealistic expectations.

"I'll tell you later"	Simple things like height, body type, and children should not fall into the tell-you-later category. The only exception to this is income; it's understandable that someone might not want to divulge his or her bracket before knowing you better.
"Intimacy," "massages," or "pleasurable"	Sensual terms are major red flags. Matches who use language filled with sexual innuendo before you meet have short-term goals.
"If you are looking for___, stop reading now"	Those who pose ultimatums before meeting are likely closed-minded about meeting matches.
"Ex"	It's too early to discuss past relationships. If it comes up before you've met, it's unlikely the match has truly moved on.
"Ready again" or "ready to move on"	If a match has to say he or she is ready, it's probably not the case.
"I don't like people who . . ."	Focusing on dislikes more than likes can indicate negative energy or an unhappy attitude.

As you can tell, most phrases involve negativity, which is always something to avoid. When projecting a first impression, you want a match to feel the warm-and-fuzzies, not that they're being fended off like a bad PC virus.

But just because you see one of these red flags does *not* mean you should eliminate a person from your flirtable queue. Depending on the individual and the context, a phrase could have an entirely different meaning. But when a few are present, it's worth considering steering clear and, instead, clicking Next to find more swoon-worthy matches.

Becoming your own customized filter is the only way to be red flag proof.

Everyone's preferences are different, and turn-offs to some are turn-ons to others. The only way to make sure you're catching all of the warning signs from a match who is lacking a little something-something is to set your own rules.

This is something I teach many of my clients, but Rachel learned it best. She and I search through matches and manage her inbox together on a weekly basis, so she's honed her filter through practice (and natural osmosis).

Taking these steps for sifting through her inbox is what helped her most:

> **Prioritize three sections.** Decide which profile sections are most important to you, and read those first. If you find red flags in those three sections, move on to the next match. For example, if it's important to you that your match lives an active lifestyle, you might want to prioritize reading the section that covers that. And if someone's answer is more about couch-surfing than surfing waves, there's an immediate strike one; one or two more, and eliminate this person from your search.

> **Know your deal breakers.** The top two or three things you could never deal with in a match should always be avoided. In Rachel's digital dating world, men who indicate a salary of less than a certain amount are the most important to avoid. She determined this from past experience. Although she dated men who were less financially successful, it always became an issue later when they discussed their future. Try to base deal breakers on experiences you don't want to duplicate. If you dated some-

one in the past who had kids and you decided afterward that you don't want stepchildren, avoid communicating with matches who have children. Take a cue from your gut, and choose two or three areas where you will absolutely not compromise.

> **Have a commonality.** If you have trouble finding common ground with your match, it can be challenging to develop a digital rapport. Make sure you have at least one thing in common, ideally two. This will help you keep eye candy at bay. When Rachel views someone's profile who appears to be a great catch but just isn't the right fit for her, she struggles to find a topic for her initial email. And let's face it, if you can't find something to compose a few lines about, that will make an impact in their inbox, it's unlikely either of you will make an impact on one another offline.

NOT ALL RED FLAGS ARE EQUAL

As someone who has seen all walks of online dating life— height, age, and zip code—let me give it to you straight on which red flags you should eliminate from your personal arsenal right away and which you should give a second look, based on the trends I notice from my clients.

> **Forty-plus, never been married.** Most of my female clients believe that men older than forty who have never been married are commitment-phobes, and they prefer to date men who are divorced or widowed instead. While some people of both sexes are avoiding the big white wedding, the majority I meet are genuine about wanting to find love. Assuming that guys in this category are damaged goods and dismissing them means you could miss out on The One.

❯ **Wants kids?** Most sites provide several options when it comes to wanting children: definitely want, want someday, maybe want, and so on. Many of my male clients, particularly those who are older than thirty-five, filter out women who don't say "definitely." Something like the desire to build a family or not is a fundamental difference and a value that you certainly need to share with your long-term love. But assuming that the "some-days" and the "maybes" are not interested without delving further is too presumptuous.

❯ **Broad preferences.** Some singles keep their preferences broad. Offline, we don't judge people for keeping their options open. But when everything is in black-and-white, we think twice. If they say they'll date someone who's twenty-five, are they really also willing to meet someone closer to their age at forty? Preferences are not deal breakers. Just because they checked off a few boxes doesn't mean they're make-or-breaks. Your matches often give less thought to these details than you would so don't automatically rule them out.

❯ **Drink "often."** If alcohol is on your list of deal breakers, by all means filter out these matches. But if it's a minor thing, keep your options open. Just because people say they drink often doesn't mean they're chugging a six-pack of Budweiser alone every Monday night.

❯ **Body type.** Determining one's own body shape can be tricky. Everyone views his or her weight differently, and it's often hard to differentiate one option from another. Some might consider an "average" girl to be "curvy" if she has a booty. But others might never search under "curvy" because they think it's code for "overweight." Ultimately, photos are more telling than a checked box. Don't get too hung up on which options your matches choose if you think they're cute. Until you meet in person, try not to overanalyze their shapes unless their bod in photos is unattractive to you.

Emails

Hesitate if you encounter inaccuracies.

Beyond red flags, there are cyber-signals that you should look out for in email communications, too. Inaccuracies are the most obvious and common. A good example of this is inconsistency between a person's profile and the first few messages they send. Your match might say in the profile that he or she is in medicine, but then you learn that the person is a medical writer. While this isn't an outright lie, small blunders can be tip-offs. If your would-be date overcompensated for his or her career, there are likely many other things also being exaggerated. And it's possible that the fibs will carry offline.

But if the inaccuracy is subtle and not an outright lie, don't automatically click the Block button. Perhaps there was a reason the match kept his or her job description vague, like being a public figure.

Age is another thing that is common to fib about, particularly for baby boomers. My client Madge is sixty-eight years old, and when she joined a dating site, she didn't receive a single message. This is unusual for women like her who are gorgeous and look young for their age. And it wasn't for lack of trying, either; she was messaging guys and getting no response. One night, she was so frustrated that she experimented by knocking a few years off her birthday. Twenty-four hours later, her profile and her inbox were getting more traffic than a highway at rush hour. She asked what I thought of the fib, and I told her that I couldn't fault her—singles older than fifty have been known to embellish their age. I know, I know, "if everyone jumped off a bridge . . ." But when tech is involved, if *everyone* your age is doing something and you don't follow the trend, you risk being filtered out and not seen or accepted by flirtables. If you find yourself in a situation like Madge's, just make sure that you don't keep your match forever in the dark. You can disclose your true age in the text of your profile or on a date.

INACCURACIES=INQUIRE

Before you delete someone from your inbox forever, use these strategies to see if things match up:

> **Share.** When you want to extract more information from a match, you first have to share a more significant part of yourself. Talking more about your own situation will make the other person more comfortable about opening up. And of course, the question you want to ask won't come out of nowhere or make you seem like you're digging too far into a topic, because you'll have already shared similar details about yourself.

> **Erase skepticism.** Genuine interest will get you the best results, so avoid negativity and confrontation. Keep the tone casual, and remove any hints of badgering. There's no need to be on the defense until you have all the facts anyway.

> **Play coy.** Remember that when you message with a match, you're flirting. So when you ask a tough question, a balanced

tone will get the best reaction. Add enough humor to keep it light, but be thoughtful enough to be taken seriously.

To give you an example, let's take a look at what Colby wrote to her latest match. She had an inkling that he was fibbing about his zip code and didn't live in her city. But rather than accuse him of the lie based on her gut feeling alone, she asked for more specific information about his favorite local spots to test his knowledge:

From: noshtosh
Sent: March 11 10:58 AM
To: artistic_poet
Subject: RE: Foodies in Seattle
. . . I also like dining out. Triple Door and the Dahlia Lounge are two of my favorite city spots. I'm particular to downtown, but as long as the ambiance and food are great, I'm there. What about you?
Jess

Taking this soft approach should give you more insight into the person you're virtually chatting with. And if the match doesn't answer, it's likely you caught him or her in a lie, and your gut red-flag reaction was right.

While you'll feel most compelled to use this approach for handling inconsistencies, you can also do this if you notice a red flag that you think might be worth looking into or that ranks as a minor offense in your personal filter book.

OFFLINE OFFENSES
Other than inconsistencies, another email red flag is a match who won't transition offline. You can't date online forever! If

you suggest meeting up and the match avoids the question or cancels plans, there might be something else going on. Deal with someone who avoids your offline advances with these solutions to keep your eFlirting on track:

> **If the match avoids getting offline,** be direct about wanting to meet. Rather than dancing around the issue, suggest a date and a time. Keep the rest of your message as short and sweet as possible so there aren't any other questions or content for the match to hide behind in a response. While this may seem too forward, let's be serious—if someone won't meet up, there's no reason to continue to communicate. Getting to the bottom of things sooner rather than later will allow you either to move on to your next click mate or finally meet this one face-to-face.

> **If the match cancels for a major reason,** such as a family issue or a last-minute trip, respond with a simple message like "No problem, hope all is OK!" Give the person some time to deal with it, and follow up a week later if he or she hasn't responded. Ask how things are, and reignite the conversation. If the person doesn't inquire about your schedule in the response, ask for plans again during your second email. If the match still doesn't agree to get beyond the broadband, then move on.

> **If the match cancels for a minor reason,** like a late night at the office or a change in plans, be understanding, but ask to reschedule right away. If the person is not ready to put you back in their calendar after a minor rescheduling snafu, he or she might not be serious about meeting.

> **If the match cancels twice,** and unless there is a very good reason for both cancellations, interest is likely waning, and it's time to move on. Don't allow anyone to string you along—focus your energy on matches who deserve your time and emails.

Offline

You might notice some red flags when you first meet up, too. There are general dating red flags—like learning that someone still lives at home at age forty or the lack of "thank you" in someone's vocabulary—but some that happen in person are specific to digital dating. When you remove the computer screens between you and your match, it's possible that you'll discover that some turn-offs remain. Here are some to be wary of when you get face-to-face:

> **Photo discrepancies.** If your match doesn't resemble his or her photos, that can be a red flag. Looking like a sister or brother to the person in the image is one thing; when you add mannerisms and new angles into the mix, it's understandable if the person is not a spitting image of the avatar you've been messaging. But if someone was clean-cut on-screen and is totally unkempt in person, it's OK to feel as if you're going to have a tough time clicking.

> **Uncover the cover-up.** If your match seems to be groping (figuratively) for answers, you might have caught your date in a fib. If someone stumbles over his or her graduation year (which reveals age), day-to-day schedule (which speaks to career), or ex-spouse details (which reveals relationship issues), it's likely that the match is trying to cover something up.

❭ Stringing you along. While the match may not cancel on you, if your plans seem to change every time you glance at your iPhone, be wary. This is a red flag for any dater, but when you haven't met yet, it's an even bigger issue. It's possible that you don't share the same level of intention. Perhaps the match is keeping you in play on the sidelines or has something to hide. Know when to cut your losses and move on to the next eBachelor or eBachelorette.

❭ Personality problem. If the person you meet in real time doesn't match the online personality, it could be that something got lost in translation. While most people are genuine about who they are, some think they need to focus more on who others want them to be. If their vibe doesn't match up to what you've been getting to know, put them on red alert.

If you read into every single nuance, you'll be limiting your digi-date potential.
Before you start getting too paranoid about what flags are red and green, remember that there is such a thing as being too analytical.

One single I know aggressively scrutinizes his matches' photos for diversity. Regardless of someone's race, he checks to make sure that her world is well rounded and judges a woman based on the friends in the photos she chooses to upload. If all of her pals are of the same race or he deems her smile "fake" in a snapshot with a person of another ethnicity, he immediately dismisses her. Clearly he had a poor experience in the past with someone who was narrow-minded, but his future matches shouldn't suffer the judgemental consequences.

Consider issues such as that one yellow flags—reasons to raise an eyebrow and make a mental note but not to eliminate a match entirely. Yellow flags are things that you can look into once you message with each other, so don't stop, just yield. If your match smiles with their mouth closed all the time, don't just assume that his or her teeth are crooked; meet up for a cup of coffee, and see for yourself. While drawing conclusions from the information available to you is reasonable, making snap judgments and dismissing someone before you have all of the material you need to make a full assessment is not. Only elevate yellow flags to red alerts after investigating. Keeping an open mind will go a long way. Ultimately, until you meet offline, your expectations won't truly take shape and solidify.

Always looking for red flags means you'll find some yellow ones, and that's OK. But the most successful online daters merely eliminate the red.

CHAPTER 9

Offline Shift

THE TRANSITION FROM DIGITAL TO DATE

Meeting offline is the single most important part of online dating. But when you meet via the interwebs, it's actually the opposite of flirting across the bar from someone. Knowing the differences will help keep your perspective in check for when you get face-to-face with a match whom you've only known message-to-message.

In traditional dating, when you make eyes at someone from across the room, it's usually because you're attracted to that person. As you chitchat, natural chemistry develops. All of the body language is there—you're leaning in, he or she is making you laugh, and after a short while, communication heats up to the point of exchanging numbers. A few days later, the person calls or texts, and you two go out on a date. What you don't know beyond your ten-minute bar-side discussion is what you have in common. Therefore, you're continuing the momentum of your connection on your date and finding out if there's enough compatibility to make getting to know the other person worth your while.

When you're dating online, you're attracted to each other's

photos, but seeing someone in person is a different experience, so chemistry is a toss-up. But compatibility is clearly in place—for example, you might both like the same museums, are career-oriented, and want kids someday. Since your relationship started based on on-screen compatibility, bridging the gap to offline chemistry can take some time to develop. It feels almost like being friends and then dating, rather than starting with a romantic spark. When you meet online, traditional dating rules need to shift to accommodate this different dynamic.

Your first encounter is not a date.
It may sound dramatic or contrary to common sense, but it's true. Traditionally, dates are opportunities to woo each other and often lead to intimacy. This is not that. Now, I'm not saying that the first time you meet won't be romantic. But to develop true chemistry, you need to experience nonverbal communication, which has remained hidden behind your screens so far. Putting away the laptops is the first step, but don't expect major fireworks to explode as soon as they click shut.

Though you've developed a rapport online, your thoughts on your match will shift when they go from 2D on a computer screen to up-close-and-personal in 3D. Some of the traits that you thought would be major parts of their vibe might be more subdued in person. And on the flip side, you may uncover some things about them that you didn't expect, but rock your world. Either way, the focus is on chemistry.

From time to time, you'll meet a match who'll be an instant connection. But in most cases, it's a slower build, because your time online was spent developing an intellectual connection while things offline are physical chemistry based. Expect sparks, not fireworks. And just as there's no guarantee that the first person you meet in a bar will be The One, you'll most likely kiss a few frogs before finding your ePrince or ePrincess.

Rather than thinking of the first time you meet as a "date," consider it a "meet-up." Changing the name in your mind will immediately keep your expectations in check by removing unrealistic romantic expectations and will remind you that if the date doesn't go well, you won't be too crushed to continue messaging and meeting others on the Wink Wide Web.

The first time my client Joan got offline with a match, she was offended that her suitor kissed her good night after a mere stroll through a museum. She thought he was cheap and ungentlemanly for not also offering to take her to dinner. But meals are second-date territory in the Winkisphere. Realizing this made her see that it actually *was* a great meet-up after all. And instead of blowing off his calls as originally intended, she called him back, and they went out for date number two later that week (entrée included).

The offline dating dynamic can take a little getting used to. Even though you shouldn't expect flowers, sweeping gestures, and being asked back to your date's place at the end of the night, you should still feel a tingle of excitement. If you're unsure of how you feel after a first meet-up, plan time to hang a second time—that date should feel a little more swoon-worthy.

This is a second first impression.
So far, your match knows you digitally inside and out. Naturally, some conclusions about you based on your profile, photos,

emails, and possibly text and/or voice messages. But meeting in person is your chance to make a second first impression.

eFlirt Byte: According to a Match.com study
of singles in America, 58 percent of men
and 51 percent of women who have been
in love and believe in love at first sight
have experienced it.

Date Night Prep

Before meeting up with a match, focus on the following three elements—look, location, and a little studying—as you primp for meeting up. These staples will ensure that you exceed expectations at the meta level.

YOUR LOOK

The first thing your match will notice about you—and the one thing he or she has been missing out on until now—is what you look like up close and in person. Regardless of how many photos you posted, meeting face-to-face is always an entirely different experience. It's an important moment, because ultimately, a lasting relationship begins with attraction. If your match can't imagine a time when he or she will want to tear off your clothes, the date probably won't go so well.

Although it's only a meet-up, make sure your look is make-out-worthy. For ladies, this means primping like you're heading out on the town; makeup and hair should reflect your Friday-night best. Outfits should be on the low-key side but still adorable, like a sundress and sparkly sandals or jeans and a cute top with heels. If you're coming straight from the office, wear a layered outfit that day so you can add va-va-voom during a quick change in the ladies' room. Removing a jacket or a cardigan, adding a statement necklace, and creating a smoky eye can take your work clothes from office-appropriate to date-chic.

Guys want to look pulled together but comfortable. So mix casual and formal elements. For example, you could don a crisp button-down (formal), dark denim jeans (casual), and nice loafers (formal). Or invert it and go with a distressed tee (casual), gray slacks (formal), and Converse sneakers (casual). If you're heading to a date spot that has a stricter dress code, just loosen up your cubicle clothes: remove your jacket, undo a button or two from your collar, and roll up your sleeves.

Regardless of gender, make sure that your look reflects your personal style. Don't wear clothes or accessories that you're not comfortable with. Meeting someone new isn't the right time to try out a new look.

LOCATION VIBE

The date location will help set the tone for your time together. While you may only be getting together for a cocktail or two, you'll want to choose a locale with flirt-worthy ambiance. Choose a spot that feels cozy and will allow you to get more comfortable with each other. Starbucks is fine and all, but candles on the tables will set you up for a stronger connection than cardboard cups.

Noise level is something else to take into consideration. You want enough energy in the space so that your first words to each other aren't overheard by the bartender but not so much that your initial exchanges get swept away with the crowd and you're forced to yell to each other.

Wine bars almost always have the right atmosphere for a first meet-up and are a great default if you're unsure of where to go (plus, it's an easy thing to search for on Yelp or Google). They're typically warm, intimate, and not too loud the way a sports bar or a jazz lounge might be.

eFlirt Byte: According to HowAboutWe, meeting for drinks never goes out of style. It's the most suggested and positively-responded-to date idea on that site.

If you or your date don't drink, independent coffee shops with a more personal vibe can be a good option. If a spot serves lattes in real mugs, it may be worth suggesting.

Of course, if you're looking to up the ante, you can get creative with your dates. Don't go too far over the top with planning, but more interesting activities are welcome. It's best if the concept is relevant to a topic of email conversation between you and your match. But if there's nothing natural, take a cue from the five most popular proposed dates on HowAboutWe: culinary adventures, shows, desserts, sightseeing, and active dates (like Frisbee or Scrabble).

When planning a meet-up, think of HowAboutWe's no-fail formula for a great first date: 1 part alcohol + 1 part activity + 1 part specific location. For example, suggest playing Ping-Pong and enjoying a craft beer at the Standard Hotel's outdoor beer garden with your match.

For specific suggestions, check out my staff's recommendations at eFlirtExpert.com/loveatfirstclick.

It's also OK to have a few tried-and-true spots, particularly for the first time you're meeting someone, since it's not uncommon to go on more first dates than second ones. Just be sure not to become a regular. My client Joe met all of his matches for the first time at the bar area of a nearby restaurant. But because he went again and again—often several times a week—the staff began to recognize him. Soon enough, his online dating luck turned. While he was going on lots of first dates, it was rare for them to turn into seconds. Obviously, something was going on, so he came to me for coaching. While he was debriefing me about his last date, he revealed that he had become chummy with a few bartenders. To him, this wasn't an issue, but I discovered that it meant a lot to his dates. The bartenders would banter with him, which not only monopolized his time but also left his potential partner disengaged and out of the loop. He was very relaxed, while she was experiencing first-date jitters. One way to ensure that you keep the focus on your match and are feeling a similar energy is to mix up locations just enough so that you're on a level playing field.

And avoid sharing a meal during the first meet-up. Committing to lunch or dinner right off the bat means you'll be on the date for a long time. Depending on the restaurant, you might have to commit to several courses, after-dinner drinks, and dessert. While this would be great for an actual date, it's too serious when you're meeting someone for the first time. Keep the activity or the date spot low-key, and graduate to something more time-consuming the next time you go out.

STUDY UP

Before you run out the door to meet your cyber-crush, be sure to review his or her profile. When you communicate online, it's easy to confuse details about matches, since you're probably chatting with multiple people simultaneously. Meeting in person will solidify who they are, but until now, you've been removed from the situation. Taking a second peek at a match's profile will give you the chance to get facts straight and the opportunity to store up conversation topics.

But you should *never* Google! Search engines are not your BFF—they won't tailor information that's relevant to your dating life, and it can be easy to misread the results. Using a search engine before you meet also elevates your level of emotional attachment, which is something that should be avoided. Getting emotionally wrapped up in your match prior to meeting only raises your expectations, which can easily turn into disappointment.

The First-Date Tango

Now that you're meeting in person, your dynamic becomes the focus of your relationship. Do you have enough common ground to exchange witty banter in real time? Can you develop chemistry with each other over time? Will this person get along with your friends?

As you establish your offline dynamic, you're setting the tone for things to come (or not, if it's not going so well). Keep yourself in check with these nine digital dating dynamic guidelines for first meet-ups:

1. Texting. When you meet offline, a text never hurts to help you find each other. When I was online dating, I used to text my date when I was almost there with a description of my outfit. This typically sparked a response about his outfit and would allow us to find each other seamlessly. Because, let's face it, one of the most awkward times can be that moment when you walk by each other. Whoops! It's nothing to be embarrassed about, because people can look totally different from their pictures. And I don't mean that they'll necessarily look worse but just, you know, different. This is a living, breathing person with mannerisms, not a Polaroid snapped in a moment anymore. So don't get text-shy when you're about to walk in the door.

2. Greeting. Meeting for the first time can be awkward. If you've done it before, you know the inevitable dance that happens between shaking hands and hugging. Oops, um, ack, sorry, OK! Awkward, right? Whether you're a lady or a gent, take the initiative and go in for a hug. It starts the vibe off on the right foot. It will serve as a reminder to you both that you're meeting on friendly and maybe even romantic terms; this is not a business meeting or a networking opportunity. It also acknowledges that you know each other already. A hug breaks the physical barrier and dives directly into pheromone-inducing territory that will allow you both to have better body language during your time together. Also, avoid common phrases like "Nice to meet you," unless your match says them first. Reminders that you haven't met yet should be avoided, since you and your match aren't strangers—you've communicated before.

3. Positioning. Nonverbal communication is crucial on a first meet-up. Sitting next to each other will enhance the likelihood that sparks will fly, so perch on a couple of barstools, lounge on a couch, or share the same side of a booth. Try to avoid sitting across from each other at a table, if possible. This will restrict body language, since you won't be able to make contact with each other as easily.

4. Touching. If you're into your match, show it. Now that you've removed the screen, it's even more important to break the ice physically. By touching a knee or a hand as you laugh, you'll build a bond beyond words, taking the way you relate to a new level. (It's much too early for a cuddle session, though.)

5. Attitude. Leave your bad day at the office behind, and focus on emitting positive vibes while you're with your match. Stress will lead to awkwardness, which won't inspire a second date for either of you. It's natural to feel a little anxiety before a date (especially if you're a first-timer), because there is still an element of the unknown. But don't let nerves get the best of you. Remember, this isn't even a date yet! You're just meeting to see if the possibility of something more exists. Avoid putting pressure on yourself, slow down your breathing to calm all that thumping in your chest, and focus on having fun.

6. Digital ceasefire. Now that you're face-to-face, remove digital devices from your relationship. That means keeping your cell in its locked position—ringer off or on vibrate. Taking a call, checking your phone, or texting during a date is a turn-off and something online daters are particularly sensitive to. You could be messaging with another match on the site's app! While all eDaters are multidating, they don't want a real-time reminder that your attention is divided. After all, you want to make sure you're in the moment.

7. Conversation. It's easy for a first meet-up to feel like a cross-examination; you've seen each other's dating résumé and likely have some questions about each other's past. Natural conversation can sometimes feel stinted by interview-like behavior. Start off your time together by asking about what is currently happening in the other person's life. Inquire about a business trip, a recent holiday, or a new recipe that they mentioned trying. Reminding the person that you already have an email rapport will make you both feel more comfortable. As much as you can, avoid the question firing range. Rather than asking question after question, expand on something he or she says by relating it to your life. Listen as much as you talk—and vice versa—and a natural flow will develop.

8. Length. The ideal first meet-up should last between forty-five and ninety minutes. To some, this may seem short, but again, this is not a traditional date. You want to figure out whether there's potential for the budding relationship and, if there is, make plans for a longer night out. Just as with other encounters in life, the energy between you during your first meeting will crescendo—it will start low, grow to a high, and then diminish. This happens when you're with pals, too, although it's much less noticeable. Everyone has experienced friend fatigue, whether after spending five hours or two straight days together. When you meet for the first time, you'll feel fatigue sooner, since your relationship is new. The decline is the worst place to leave your match. You want to leave someone inspired to see you again, not longing for the safety of his or her own couch. The key is to wrap up the date when you feel that the energy between you has hit its peak. If the date isn't going well, the other person is weird or doesn't resemble his or her photo, or conversation isn't flowing, don't be afraid to ditch politely after thirty to forty-five minutes. Common etiquette for these meet-ups requires you to stay at least that long—and make sure you do. Sometimes awkwardness will dissipate over time. But if it's clear that there's no spark, make your excuse and jet.

9. Exit. Wrapping up a date should be seamless, although this can be tough to achieve. Having plans for right after your meet-up helps, because you'll have somewhere to be at a specific time, and your match can't really say or do anything to keep you longer. If you don't have other plans, you can always mention another activity that you need to get home to, whether it's finishing up a work presentation or letting a pet out. For a parting gesture, do whatever feels most comfortable: a hug or a peck on the cheek, or, if the vibe's right, go in for a frenchie.

After You Meet Up, Follow Up

Whatever you do, avoid reverting to your dating site roots. Once you've met face-to-face, keep the relationship offline—no excuses. Almost all of my clients who are online dating virgins want to return to the comforts of the dating site to continue chatting, but there are few things that can kill a dynamic quicker than putting firewalls around your pending relationship.

For Amber, it almost proved to be the demise of the momentum she had going with Tate. They had one of those whirlwind first dates where the chemistry was palpable. They talked nonstop, stayed for several cocktails, made plans to see each other again, and ended the night with a kiss straight out of a rom-com. He texted her right after, and they continued texting back and forth all the way home. But the next day, she followed up with a message on the site, and things began to unravel. Amber never heard back from him and called me in a panic. Immediately, I knew that he hadn't responded because tech got in her way. The truth is, messaging through the site after meeting can be unpredictable. You don't know when your match's next log-in will be, and you risk getting buried in his or her incoming mail from new potentials. It's better placement to ping his or her phone, either with a call or a text, so you're not competing with new matches. After all, you already like each other offline. If you're chatting through another form of digital communication such as texting, it's OK, because it's a real-time environment. This way, conversation can unfold more naturally. Of course, the ultimate goal is to integrate this person into your regular life and vice versa, so using everyday modes of communication will help facilitate this transition seamlessly.

But what you say after your first meet-up, how proactive you are about initiating conversation, and where you communicate will differ depending on how you feel. I've noticed that both sexes are hesitant about the follow-up and are confused about what platform to use. Most people assume that a call is always the best way to go, no matter what. But direct-dialing your match doesn't always give you the win. Let's determine which approach to take by first evaluating how the date made you feel.

DEFINITE LIKE

If your match puts a bounce in your step and you're ready to add date number two to your calendar, follow up the next morning with a thank you. Not only is it polite, but it also sends good vibes and encourages conversation. If your communication style has been strictly digital (say, you've never spoken on the phone before), send a message via text. While it may seem impersonal, texting is a great way to have short conversations that grows your relationship dynamic and continues an ongoing dialogue. We'll go into more detail on flirting via your mobile in chapter 11, but keeping communication in cyberspace at this point will make you both feel more comfortable, allowing for a flirty comfort factor. Don't worry if the conversation peters out; this first step is simply to show appreciation and establish an open line of communication.

> eFlirt Byte: According to JDate, 28 percent of
> singles surveyed said that if their dates don't
> bother to call, they shouldn't bother at all.

Guys, when you're ready to ask your match out again, call to show genuine interest. Trust me, she'll appreciate the extended gesture. But ladies, if he doesn't make plans, don't fret. As long as he continues to communicate with you, he's interested, so nudge the conversation in the offline direction, or simply ask him out yourself. If you've been chatting only via text so far, keep the mode of communication the same, since you're already making a bolder-than-average move.

MAYBE

I encourage singles who are in the gray area about a date to go out with their matches again. If your first meet-up left you feeling so-so, you'll have a clearer idea after a second date whether your maybe match is a definite or a no way. Meeting again will give you peace of mind that you're giving each potential a fair opportunity to tug at your heartstrings, and a second meet-up also means that you'll avoid that "what if" feeling in the future.

If you're unsure about your first date, go casual with the follow-up. Give it a few days, send a quick text to say hi, and see what develops. If your match doesn't follow up with a message, let it drop. But if text chitchat ensues, make plans.

NO THANKS

When your date doesn't go as planned and there's absolutely no chance you'll want another, give the match the silent treatment. Online daters are typically dating multiple people, so consider this one a blip on the radar, and let him or her move on without going through a too-soon breakup—after all, you only went out once! But if your match follows up, you'll need to bare it all rather than string your date along. You can send the match to voicemail, but you do need to close the eFlirting loop. Compose a message through the dating site and deliver the news the same way you would with an online match devoid of digital sparks: thank, decline, wish well. Keeping your communication on the site rather than by text or phone will deter the match from being persistent.

Now Traditional Courtship Reigns

Once you've decided to continue seeing each other, you can expect a more typical dynamic to evolve. The second, third, and fourth dates will lay the foundation for a relationship, and your date spots should reflect that. On the second date, do something that requires a bit more of a time investment, like dinner. Continuing conversation is a must, so if you're going to do something like a movie, make sure you also spend time together either before or after sans quiet zone. You'll be able to get a better feel for your match and have more time to connect and develop chemistry.

For date three, pick an activity. Doing fun things together will create a memory, which means a new kind of bond between you. Your match will forever associate you with that amazing day spent picking apples, seeing a free concert, or cooking *coq au vin*. This will also allow both you and your match to see how you might fit into each other's life. For example, if your kitchen time together is full of flour wars, you've learned that you can be goofy around each other. But if, instead, you end up arguing over ingredients, you may want to think twice about how you'll relate to each other in the long run.

It's inevitable that you're going to have some bad dates along the way—that's life, whether you meet online or at your local watering hole. Just leave the bad experiences behind and say, "On to the next!" Saying *sayonara* to the ones who aren't the best fits will remove negativity from your life and keep you focused on matches with potential.

CHAPTER 10

Online Dating Blues

MOVING PAST FRUSTRATION

Online dating can sometimes get intense. If you get burned out from dating in real life, you simply stop sending out signals that you're available and focus on yourself, friendship, and maybe even work. But the Web doesn't shut itself down. Your profile is working for you 24/7, 365. That's often a huge advantage—you can be *sleeping* and still be a full screen flirt, receiving messages from matches. But there are a million things online that can get under an eDater's skin. Here are a few that you might have already experienced and how you should think about them to get past the online dating blues.

> **Pretty, pretty dater.** With potentially millions of singles on a particular site—rather than, say, fifty people in a bar—being digitally dashing takes serious thought and effort. As a result, you may find yourself constantly worrying: Am I projecting the right image? What can I be doing better? What do people think when they see my profile?

Reality check: With the click of a mouse, you can change your online actions. This means that you're more in control of your own dating destiny. Use it to your advantage.

❭ **"Rejection."** With more singles logged on, there's more potential, but there's also more competition. You might be sending a lot of messages, but you won't get a response to each one. So it's easy to feel more down on yourself than you would otherwise.

Reality check: You're reaching out more, so receiving fewer responses is natural. And your matches are making judgments based on a singular profile on a computer screen—so they cannot truly "reject" or "accept" until they meet you.

❭ **Mr. or Ms. Wrong.** A large user base on a site can also mean being contacted by all the wrong people. But seeing more and more matches enter your inbox that are not right for you can also take a toll on your heart.

Reality check: Sometimes simple shifts in your profile or preferences can keep these unsavory matches at bay. But just like at a bar, any member can approach you. If you've made some changes and you're still getting negative matches in your inbox, stop fretting, and delete them. Whom you choose to message is way more important than those who come through your inbox unsolicited.

❭ **Tick-tock.** Sometimes online dating can be as time-consuming as a part-time job. When you're proactive, you might get frustrated, feeling as if you're spending more time than necessary to set up dates.

Reality check: If you meet The One online, it will all be worth it.

〉 The waiting game. Since most online dating sites involve waiting for responses and working around other people's schedules, your dating mojo can lag. Many clients I meet with have very specific goals; for example, Joel wanted a date for the weekend of his fortieth birthday. While I understood why he wanted companionship to reach a milestone, it's not always realistic to target a specific two-day window for a date when you don't know what your flirting future together holds. To complicate matters, sharing a weekend with a first date would be strange, so he would have needed to go out with the person a few times first. Experiencing such a personal milestone with someone you won't see again would be even more disappointing than being dateless.

Reality check: Throw your time-specific goals out the window so you don't disappoint yourself and feel blue because you weren't able to achieve them.

〉 Same old, same old. Seeing the same matches over and over again—regardless of what site you join—can bring your spirits down. This is a particularly common challenge for singles residing in smaller communities and for mature daters. In both situations, quantity in the community is lacking, so naturally, site populations are smaller.

Reality check: This will push you to date outside your comfort zone, often leading you to find potential where you might otherwise not. While you may consider a long list of options a benefit, remember that if you're looking for a long-term relationship, it only takes One!

Even when you're armed with this information, it's inevitable that you'll feel discouraged after months of logging in, dozens of emails from the wrong matches, and a handful of disaster dates. Your mind will spin, and at some point, variations of these unhealthy thoughts will begin:

Online dating doesn't work.
Why am I doing this, anyway?
I've wasted so much time.

Let me give you a few other thoughts to focus on:

This is normal.
You are OK.
Anything worth having takes time.

Before throwing your laptop out the window, let's put some of your negative thoughts into perspective.

Online dating doesn't work. Literally hundreds of thousands of couples meet online. While it may seem daunting, remember that dating on the Web is a process similar to dating in real life. Just because the initial encounter is different doesn't mean the outcome will be. It still takes time, energy, and a little bit of heartache—just like meeting matches offline.

> eFlirt Byte: According to *U.S. News & World Report,* forty million people search for love online each month.

Why am I doing this, anyway? In today's digital world, "putting yourself out there" means dating online and off. One without the other simply isn't being proactive enough. You might meet your next date at the grocery store or a restaurant, but you might also meet him or her on a dating site or through a social network like Facebook. Online dating also gives you the opportunity to opt-in to finding someone and have options when you might not otherwise. After all, you don't go out *every* night, right?

I've wasted so much time. It's easy to feel as if the last few months have been a loss, but remember that you've been learning throughout your journey. Not only have you developed digital swagger, but you've also learned so much about yourself. Knowing your preferences and going on dates—even when they were more "miss" than "hit"—are an important part of being able to recognize The One when he or she appears full screen. Even with seemingly efficient methods and hundreds of potential suitors at your fingertips, online dating is not a quick fix if you're looking for a long-term partner.

If you find that venting is your preferred method for a healthy mindset, join BadOnlineDates.com, a social community for eDaters. You can gripe about your latest date and remind yourself that you're not alone in your online dating journey. But if you still can't keep your cool, shut down and reboot. While pushing through your temporary tough spot without taking a break might seem like a good idea, it can have its consequences. All too often, clients who don't heed my suggestion to take time off risk doing permanent damage to their online dating life.

A few months ago, I got an email from my client Ben. After I'd been working with him for more than eight months, he messaged me his "success" story. Usually, when a client enters into a relationship, I jump for joy, but this one left me staring blankly at the screen. Even though he was delivering the news that he was in a relationship, his tone was unabashedly depressed. His new girlfriend didn't fit any of his three most important criteria.

She wasn't Jewish (his *only* deal breaker was that she share his faith), she lived very far from him (he had already experienced a challenging long-distance relationship prior to dating online), and she had financial issues (Ben was a stickler about saving). He acknowledged that she wasn't perfect but wanted to see how things played out.

I'm all about dating outside the box, but I'm not for accepting deal breakers. I was disappointed in his decision, but I also knew that it was a result of his online dating burnout. Dating depression can coerce you into making decisions you wouldn't otherwise.

The opposite can happen, too; you could end up so frustrated with your love life that you overlook a potential click mate. Luckily, I was able to stop this from happening with my client Georgia. She was so aggravated with the online dating process that she kept declining dates. But I was able to persuade her to meet up with a guy I felt would be a good fit for her. Despite the fact that her hatred for me grew deeper, she put on her little black dress, wiped the pout off her face, and strutted to the wine bar as planned. The next day, my phone was unusually silent—no morning-after call to reenact her femme-fatale evening. But a week later, Georgia called to fill me in on her budding relationship. She had seen him three times already, and I could tell he was the soon-to-be love of her life.

Georgia had my encouragement to push her out the door and on to the date, but she could have easily overlooked him entirely. As the online dating blues grab hold, it's common to find yourself becoming more and more selective. But if you're feeling down, a date might be just the thing to perk you up. Even if the date isn't perfect, a glimmer of hope can help lift your spirits up.

eFlirting Sleep Mode

Taking a break isn't a sign of weakness, and it will set you up for a better experience. I recommend that you walk away from your monitor if you're upset with online dating for more than three consecutive weeks. Follow these four steps to powering down temporarily so you can develop a fresh perspective.

1. Check your recent conversations. If you're in the middle of an email string with a match or two and are close to getting offline, don't log off yet. While it's possible to pick up where you left off, if you take a long break, your cyber-crush could be in a relationship by the time you return. Giving out your number to these matches is the best course of action. It will still feel as if you're taking a break from online dating, because you won't need to sign in to communicate with them, and it will typically hustle along the process to meeting offline. Let them know that you're taking a break from your membership but that you'd still love to meet.

2. Back up info. Some sites delete messages after a certain amount of time, so if there are matches with whom you're in the beginning stages of communicating, copy and paste their usernames and email strings into an offline archive to make sure that your history with your crush is saved. Documenting this information on your own hard drive will allow you to pick up where you left off later on if the matches you were communicating with are still members of the site.

3. Know your subscription details. Before you let your activity on a paid dating site lag, make sure you set a calendar reminder for the next renewal date. Most sites default to auto-renewing your account. This can be turned off before you leave the site, but keeping the auto-renew on is actually a good thing; it will force you to make a conscious decision when your calendar pings you about whether you're ready for your break to end.

4. Duck and cover. It may be tempting to give up completely—delete your account and erase every memory of your virtual love life. But feeling down shouldn't equal waving the white flag. Would you give up on dating in real life altogether? Rather than deleting your account, simply deactivate it, which will allow you to hide your profile. Although your profile will be completely inactive, your data won't be lost. And returning after your break will be as simple as clicking a button.

No log-ins allowed during your break. You will be tempted to sign in, particularly during those lonely nights when you wish you had a BF or GF to snuggle with under the duvet, but staying free and clear will refresh your mind-set. Set a time minimum for your break. That way, you'll stay offline for at least a specific amount of time to give your heart's hard drive a break. It should be no shorter than two weeks, but for most singles, it's a few months.

In the meantime, focus on yourself during this time, just as you would after a breakup. Take yourself on dates, and indulge in activities you haven't done in a while. Whether you go on a road trip, join a soccer league, or spend time with friends, you'll boost your self-confidence and start feeling like you again. Later, you'll be more ready to meet your match. Above all, focusing on yourself and not others will take you out of that frustrating head space and remind you who's in control.

When your calendar alerts you that your break is over, make a decision either to extend it or to rejoin the online dating community. Extending your break is completely normal. So if you're still feeling down, don't force yourself to return. Select a later time, and reevaluate where you stand; that way, you can determine if you're ready without pressure.

Makin' a Comeback

When you *are* ready to log back on, it's most important to keep a positive mind-set; otherwise, your break would have been all for nothing! Reenter the Wink Wide Web by refreshing your online behaviors to match your renewed outlook. Doing each of these four steps is essential to your digital dating health.

1. Check out new sites. Your previous online dating experience may have been only so-so because you weren't part of the right community. Different sites attract different personalities, so log on to a few new sites, and noncommittally check out your matches before subscribing. Even if you did like your past site, there's something to be said for trying something new in addition to your old virtual stomping ground (even if it's only for one month).

2. Refresh your profile. Before reactivating your eFlirting presence, revisit your profile. At the very least, upload a few photos that were taken recently. This can attract a whole new group of matches. To give yourself a true eMakeover, update the text, too.

3. Remove expectations. While it's great to make online dating part of your everyday routine and to have a goal for what you will accomplish, avoid milestones that you're not in control of, such as specific numbers of incoming messages or dates per week. This risks setting you up for disappointment, which will likely be challenging to handle after a break.

4. Re-evaluate your preferences. After some "me" time and soul searching, you'll probably have a clearer image of the type of person you want to meet. This should be reflected in your profile and preferences, but keep it part of your approach, too. When you begin reviewing matches' profiles again for the first time, keep this in the forefront of your mind to make sure that you're pursuing the right type.

Taking a breather from online dating when you're feeling burned out is a necessity, as is returning with the proper mindset. Don't judge yourself based on your breaks—if you need to take a month or so off every season or so, that's OK. Everyone takes a different journey through online dating.

CHAPTER 11

Sexy Textie

FLIRTING VIA YOUR MOBILE

Whether you have an iPhone, an Android, a BlackBerry— or are still toting around an old-school flip phone— eFlirting extends to your mobile screen, too. In our apped-up, textaholic world, being digitally savvy means being in the mobile know. Forget the formal phone call; whether you are college-age or retirement-bound, using your thumbs to communicate is an essential twenty-first-century dating skill.

> eFlirt Byte: According to a Pew Internet study,
> 3.5 million text messages are sent
> every minute in the U.S.

Texting is the most common way to use your cell to communicate on the go. It's natural to feel as if your match is being short with you if you've mainly communicated on a dating site until now, where messages are more formal and lengthy. The more real-time the communication, the shorter and more casual the response you can expect.

The Texting Style Guide

It's important to realize that just as there are different verbal communication styles, there are also different kinds of texting styles. Whether you're a novice or a pro, let's break them down so you can focus on how to use your smartphone and your match's eCommunication style to your advantage.

> The check-in. Quick conversations that happen via text message are check-ins. They typically start off with a simple "hi" or an inquiry about how you are and don't expand much beyond that. But even if the conversation doesn't progress, your match is letting you know that you're on his or her mind and that he or she is still into you.

Tip: If your match is into checking in, make sure to give some check-in sugar back so it's not completely one-sided. And if you're the one initiating this style, make sure that you also occasionally strike up a more lengthy conversation.

> The banter. Conversation that isn't necessarily important but keeps your blossoming relationship on its toes is banter. (Hint: If you text periodically about day-to-day happenings, you're bantering with your match.) There often isn't a beginning, a middle, and an end to a conversation; it just seems to flow over the course of the day and, possibly, from one day to the next.

Tip: If you favor bantering, make sure to ease into this style with a new match. Jumping into long text discussions after only a first date can overwhelm someone who still doesn't know you too well. Keep it light, slowly amping up the repartee, paying attention to the digital signals the match is sending you. If the person starts responding more quickly, that's a good sign that he or she is into your text chitchat. And if your match banters, make sure you keep up! When you're busy, it's OK to keep your answers shorter; just be sure to slip your pending meeting or drive to the supermarket casually into conversation so the match will understand your response time.

〉 The date update. Some eDaters prefer to keep digital communication to a minimum. (Don't worry; we'll get into the call-versus-text debate later.) At a minimum, though, texting makes planning convenient. Let your match know you're running a few minutes behind schedule, communicating the address of your date spot, or making a change in the evening's plans—when the information is minor like this, it's easier to text than to call, since the aim isn't a conversation. Being a scheduler shows your match that you are being thoughtful and want to have the best time possible.

Tip: Schedule-only texts are impersonal, so go one step further by mentioning your excitement about seeing your match. This lets the person know that even though you're keeping your texts short and sweet, you're not just emotionlessly going through the dating motions.

〉 The sext. Back in the chat room days, singles would "cyber"—have virtual sex through words on a screen in real time. But the new-school version happens via your smartphone. Sexting involves discussing the act of sex, often with the inclusion of scantily clad photos.

Tip: Of all of the communication styles, the sext is the one that requires both you and your match to have an equal comfort level—particularly since getting digital and dirty can escalate to s-e-x. If your match begins to sext and you're not ready to go there, feign shyness, restrict your answers to only a few characters, and brush off the X-rated language.

eFlirt Byte: An LG Text Ed study found that
59 percent of people ages twenty to twenty-six
have engaged in some kind of sexting.

Texting 101

Don't worry—while you and your match may have conflicting text styles, you should be able to find common ground. Just as with other aspects of a relationship, you'll need to compromise. If your match is a banterer and you'd prefer to only text updates about your plans, meeting in the middle—particularly in the beginning of your relationship—will ensure that technology doesn't become a stumbling block to romance.

Some hesitate more than others before they hit the Send button, but regardless of comfort level, there are universal rules to use when sending or receiving texts with a click mate.

〉 First-timer hello. If you haven't texted with your match yet, make sure to sign your name at the end of the message. On the off chance that your match hasn't entered you into his or her contacts, you want to make sure it's clear who's striking up a textie dialogue.

〉 Beware the drunken text. Texting under the influence should be avoided at all costs; it can lead to major embarrassment later. You might contact an ex, reach out to someone you're no longer into, or ruin a good thing by revealing information you'd otherwise keep private. If you plan on having one too many cocktails, either turn off your phone or give it to a responsible friend. This will save you from day after 'splaining.

> **Review before sending.** As you've learned in chapters 3 and 4, you're often judged by what you write. So grammar and spell-check are still important when texting. With the advent of auto-correct, simple texts can get complicated. Complete the whole message and reread before hitting Send to avoid miscommunication that will make you shake your fist and yell, "Damn you, auto-correct!"

> **Know who is on the other end.** Texting makes it easy to communicate with multiple people. But make sure that efficiency doesn't result in relationship ruin—multitexting means it's easy to message the wrong person by accident. My client Alyssa was psyched when she got a message from a date she was crushin' on . . . until she realized it was meant for another lady. Needless to say, she called out the would-be gent on his text etiquette and decided not to schedule another date.

> **After ten.** Beyond a certain hour, texting can enter booty-call territory. Texting late night is fine, but if your match tries to set up an impromptu in-person appearance after ten P.M., it's probably for more than a cup of coffee. If you're not cool with hooking up sans wining and dining, either skip the late-night texts or seem busy when your match virtually knocks on your door.

> **Keep conversation light.** Texting is a way to keep the relationship moving along, but it is not a medium to dispense serious news. Avoid asking or answering serious questions via text.

You'll need more characters than is customary, anyway, so stick to banter.

❭ Avoid text floods. Being persistent is one thing, but flooding your match with messages is another. Avoid sending back-to-back messages when your match hasn't responded. If you're in mid-conversation, it will be overwhelming to receive many alerts at once. If you need to explain a point further, it's OK to break the rules by sending two messages in a row but no more than that. And if your match has gone silent on the message string, sending another text when you haven't received a reply to the first will come off as badgering. If your match goes completely silent, see the "Troubleshoot Texts" section below for how to handle this situation.

❭ Keep your phone out of sight on dates. Text etiquette extends to offline behavior, too. While you're on a date, your phone should remain in your pocket or purse. Responding to a message or taking a call is rude. Focus on your match until you part ways—even if you don't think he or she is The One.

❭ Time between texts. Don't be an eager beaver; if your match hasn't responded in a couple of hours, it's not an excuse to call in the National Guard. Don't stress about slow responders. Just because you're sitting by your phone doesn't mean your match is, too. But make sure to follow your match's lead. If he or she takes six hours to write back, don't respond within one minute. Give it ten or twenty minutes before replying but don't keep them waiting (and wanting) for too long. If you have the person's attention, you want to keep it. After an hour they may not be available again.

❭ **The thank-you text.** If texting is a major mode of communication for you, it's customary to text words of appreciation to your match after a date. You can either do this an hour or so after you part ways or the next day. Whether you're a guy or a gal, this step will signal to your matches that not only are you polite, but you're also into them.

❭ **Maintain your voice.** Your texts should sound just like you, only digital. So don't change your vibe. If you're well spoken in person, eliminate acronyms and abbreviations in your virtual-speak. If you're straightforward, don't suddenly go all gushy with romantic eGestures. And if you're upbeat and free-spirited, maintain that energy in your texts.

There Is Subtext in Texts

You can't always take a text at face value. What your match types isn't always as black-and-white as it comes across on your phone's screen. The key to enlightening yourself is to reread. So if you're in doubt, read and then read again. Here is a quick conversation from Lorraine's phone that demonstrates this point:

> *L:* Running a few minutes late. Be there soon!
> *Date:* Oh. OK well how late? Just got a table.
> *L:* Only 5. See you soon!
> *Date:* OK!

While this seems like a simple scheduling conversation, her date is definitely a little peeved. "Just got a table" is a subtle "hurry the hell up." While he's trying to reflect her enthusiasm with an exclamation, it's faux excitement. Lorraine said that he was a little "off" when they met up, but they seemed to get back onto the same page over time, and luckily, the night went well. Since Lorraine was aware of the subtext of his text, she arrived better prepared to get her date back on track.

Troubleshoot Texts Met with Silence

If your date goes quiet during a text string, it doesn't automatically signal disinterest. Similar to messaging on a dating site, every scenario is different. But just like online, there are many reasons for silence. So before you delete a name from your iPhone or Droid forever, let's call in eFlirt IT:

> **Review priors.** Start by reviewing your past communications, if any. Read between the lines, and make sure there wasn't a cue you missed that might have made him or her digitally bristle. It's also possible that your match may be skimping on responses because he or she is just not comfortable with your level or style of communication.

> **Wait it out.** Even if sending another text seems aggressive, you should go for it. Since texting is so casual, you never know if your message simply fell off the radar because he or she has been busy. But wait three days before you hit Send. If your post-date thank-you text was met with silence, the avoidance could have been a fluke, but it could also mean that your match is not interested. Before you go jumping to conclusions, follow-up so you know for sure. You'll have either closure or another date.

> **Notice what time it is.** Just because you're free to text doesn't mean your crush is. For example, some prefer not to text during

business hours. When your match goes silent, try texting another day at a different time to see if you get a response. After a while, you and your match will know what texting times work for both of you.

> **Vary content.** Change up your texting strategy the second time around. Bring up a new topic, and make sure to ask a question. If your match is interested, inquiring about something should get him or her talking just as it would in an initial email. Make sure that you're asking open-ended (and casual) questions. Yes-or-no questions won't get the conversation flowing, and you risk hitting another dead end with your match.

> **Mode of communication.** If you've only briefly texted together before, your match's one-word answers or silence might be a sign that texting isn't the preferred method of communication.

While navigating unanswered texts can be a challenge, the opposite can happen, too. My client Serena set up a date a week out, but her match started blowing up her phone with messages right away. His texts seemed weird, not only because they hadn't met yet but especially because his banter arrived midday, when she was busy at work. Although she was turned off by it, Mr. Text-Happy's mobile behavior wasn't a deal breaker. I encouraged her to wait until much later in the evening, say nine P.M., before responding noncommittally. Her message said, "Had a busy one as I'm sure you can tell! Hope yours was great. G'night."

This approach sends the virtual message that you're too busy to chat in the daytime and closes off the conversation nicely. The match should get the hint and quit it with the predate texting. If not, then you might consider the behavior a deal breaker.

When You've Gotta Call

Sometimes you've got to get voice-to-voice. While texting is great, there are some instances when it's absolutely necessary to pick up the phone and say hello. In the texting-versus-calling debate, both camps have strengths—and believe it or not, they may not be as age-specific as you think. Most of the singles I meet assume that people who are younger prefer texting and those who are older want to call. But it's important not to pre-judge your match's method of communication based on age alone.

My client Vicky is a forty-one-year-old executive. The first time I suggested that she should call her match about a more serious matter rather than texting, she told me she would *never* just call someone on the phone without scheduling it first. To her, calling is "too intrusive."

But on the flip side, Kristin, a twenty-two-year-old med student, prefers dates to call. She balked at the suggestion of texting to check-in. In fact, she disabled texting from her phone plan altogether so guys were forced to call.

A mixture of these modes of communication is a good thing for your relationship. In a handheld world, disabling text functionality is dangerous if everyone is not in the know on your phone plan particulars. Think of all the messages you might miss! But it's definitely important to be aware of what works best for what . . . and for whom. Use whichever mode of communication is most comfortable for you, but keep in mind what your match prefers. If your match's cell-phone plan has a maximum amount of minutes, it might be better to keep the marathon conversations under wraps and put your thumbs to work more, or vice versa. A match might be head-over-heels for you but wouldn't want to have a sky-high bill, either.

There are three topics of communication that should never be approached digitally:

1. Something serious. If you need to discuss a serious or emotional subject, dial your match's digits. Having a heated debate via texts is a major no-no. You'll likely misinterpret each other's words, and you risk your match taking the conversation too casually.

2. Asking someone out. Once you've had your first date, singles—especially women—prefer being asked out in a more personal way. So give a call to ask her out and make plans. It should be faster than texting back and forth, anyway. This rule is not always followed by the masses, so don't be disappointed if someone doesn't dial your number. If chatting about the date is important to you, just type a gentle hint, such as "Sure, give me a call and let's chat through the details."

3. Long stories. Anything that requires a description of more than 160 characters should happen voice-to-voice. Have you ever tried to read a novel on your cell? Not easy. So either just text the highlights or save the story for your next phone call or date.

Flirting Is Sexting's Foreplay

There is a fine, very gray line between sexting and flirting. Cross it at the wrong place and the wrong time, and your relationship could go from sexy to skanky in two seconds flat. Just as you wouldn't move from a batted eyelash to a roll in the sheets, there has to be some heavy ePetting before you can climax to sexting.

Texting doesn't always lead to sexting, but if getting digitally bare is your modus operandi, begin by playing coy, using double entendres, and sending playful yet sexy messages. This will allow you to get a little cozier with each other's comfort level before taking things further. You'll know your match is responding well when he or she joins in. If all signs are a go, make the transition to sexting by mentioning turn-ons and desires. And if your match reciprocates with his or her own, amp up your sexts by describing what you'd do together, mentioning favorite body parts and scenarios where your guy or gal is the star of your fantasy.

YOUR SEXTING PLAYBOOK

To stay on the right side of seduction, follow these six digital-nookie rules:

1. Meet in real time first. There should be no sexting before you've met offline. If your date takes initial conversations into sexual territory, it should be a huge red flag. You don't even know if you're attracted to each other in person yet! So unless you're looking for a fling rather than a date, keep interactions PG-13.

2. Read responses. If there is subtext in all texts, it's amplified in sexting. Although getting digital and dirty can be fun, it also leaves more opportunities for misunderstandings. Make sure to read everything twice before you respond, and take your time crafting your reply.

3. Sex before sext. If you're not 100-percent comfortable with virtually pushing your match's buttons yet, wait until you see skivvies in person. Once you've bared it all, you'll likely feel more empowered to start up a convo in the cloud and be less self-conscious. Prefacing sex with the digital version comes off as too aggressive when initiated by men. But confident ladies can use it to build sexual tension, with the understanding that the next time you see each other, you'll move your relationship under the sheets.

4. Text first, sext later. Make sure you know that your match is around and reading your messages before you send something revealing through the cell towers. It's important to know that your match is actively looking at your texts, because if he or she were to read your sext hours later, it might be an inappropriate time and a turn-off.

5. Delete conversations. While it may be fun to look back on old sext strings, storing them in your phone isn't exactly safe keeping. Archiving a date's number is one thing, but you don't want to risk your past sexts getting to the wrong person, like your joker friends or the maitre d' from last night. You never know what's going to happen to your phone, so be safe, not sorry. To motivate yourself to hit Delete, clearly imagine the moment when your new BF or GF stumbles upon sexts from your ex. And don't be afraid to talk to your partner about taking similar precautions.

6. Leave an air of mobile mystery with photos. Pictures to go along with the storyline will enhance the experience. But there is such a thing as leaving your sexter-with-benefits wanting more. If your date hasn't seen you in the nude yet, let him or her experience you in the flesh before you begin snapping photos. Until then, your words are enticing enough. If you do send photos, make sure you trust the person on the other end of the dial pad, and be sure to crop out your face so you'll have more deniability if they wind up in the wrong hands.

eFlirt Byte: According to LG Text Ed, nearly one in five sext recipients have passed a sext along to someone else.

Beyond Texting: Your Mobile as a Flirting-Management Tool

When you're dating online, you may have more short-term relationships than usual. This is OK, since, as discussed in chapter 9, the first time you meet is *not* a date. But as a result, your cell contacts can get a little messy.

Let's face it, saving numbers in your phone is a digital art. Follow my guidelines for contact entry so you won't confuse those three Matts in your phone.

❯ Identify by dating site. Keep your matches straight by adding the first letter of the dating site you met on. For example, "E" for eHarmony and "O" for OkCupid. This will not only help jog your memory, but it will also signal that you met digitally. When someone texts or calls, you'll know exactly the nature of your relationship, even if the first Nancy who jumps to mind is your aunt. Until you learn the person's last name, this can be entered in place of his or her last initial. And after you learn the full name, you can add the dating site indicator after the surname.

> **Names you can't pronounce.** Every once in a while, you'll come across a Javier or a Rajesh. Do as the professional announcers do, and add the phonetic spelling to your contact list. Follow it up with the real spelling so you won't forget their on-paper identity.

> **Add details.** Nearly all Smartphones will allow you to add any contact field you wish. Scroll to the bottom of the contact form, and enter your match's birthday, the date you met, his or her username, and anything else your heart desires. Just be wise with your wireless decisions—adding uncensored notes on your date could backfire if that person ever views the entry, so include necessary facts only.

> **Take them out of rotation.** If things don't go so well with a match, wait a month, and then edit the contact information by switching the person's name to "do not answer" or something silly like "pudgemuffin," the nickname you and your friends dubbed your date. Removing someone entirely from your list is a no-no, because if he or she contacts you months later, you won't know who it is and might be tempted to ask.

> **Ring tones.** Even if pop songs aren't your thing, you can use different standard ring and text tones to give you an auditory cue. One tone for matches you dig will advise you to pick up

immediately, while another for old flames will remind you to let the call go to voicemail.

Remember, virtual talk adds to your relationship dynamic, so be mindful of your textual behavior. Take your time with mobile communicado—because you're still screen-to-screen. While it may be easy to delete a moment from your memory, you can't unsend a digital declaration.

CHAPTER 12

Pop-Tech Flirting

EMBRACING NEW DIGITAL DATING TOOLS

Up to this point, we've tackled the ins and outs of traditional online dating. But there are so many different ways to court your crush via the Web. In fact, the digital dating industry is constantly evolving, with new forms of popular technology that launch every other week. Lucky for you, I'm not one to sit on the sidelines. As an early adopter, I'm constantly downloading apps, logging on to sites, giving singles demos on how to use them, and meeting with founders to get the inside scoop on their upcoming releases. Right now, there are three main revolutions in the pop-tech evolution: startups, mobile apps, and social media flirting.

Startup Approaches

Society is embracing an affinity for "newisms"—the latest, greatest, most innovative *everything*. And this is especially true in tech. Whether it's the newest release of the iPhone or the latest social media platform, consumers crave having digital creativity at their fingertips. But newism technology launches fast and furious, and only consumers determine which sites and apps will hit it big—and which will fall by the wayside.

> eFlirt Byte: Draw Something, a social-gaming
> app, acquired 35 million users in
> only three weeks.

In the dating realm, consumers' craving for new tech means fresh concepts for connecting. Startups and corporations have a place in the dating industry, and logging on to platforms created by both will strengthen your dating life. The more you open up your tech world, the more tools you have, and the more matches you'll meet!

WHAT'S TRENDING

New developments are happening all the time. In fact, there's probably a programmer sitting at a laptop coding the next best thing as we speak. Here are some innovative genres that are currently all the digi-date rage:

❯ **Group-dating sites.** Removing the one-on-one aspect of dating, these sites allow you to meet in pairs or small groups. You connect online over group profiles or are set up blind. When you all meet, you'll eventually pair off one-on-one throughout the evening in a more organic way, like when you're meeting friends of friends.

❯ **Daily curations.** To some, being innovative with the search process means eliminating the log-in. Instead, they send one featured match per day directly to all of their users' personal email addresses.

❯ Friend of a friend. Attempting to digitize the in-person process of introducing two single friends to each other and playing matchmaker, these sites typically sync with your social media presence. Utilizing Facebook Connect, you can be involved even if you're in a relationship by matching your friends up.

❯ Social connect. A lot of new technology is built entirely off of the social grid. Whether it's matching you with Twitter followers or Foursquare users, your virtual friends—even the ones you've never met in person—might make their way to an in-person connection. Some of these technologies also use your social media preferences to introduce you to those outside your current digital circle.

❯ Facial recognition. Rather than matching based on interests or personality, some sites pair users up based on their similar facial features. The basis for sites like these is research showing that we often have chemistry with those whose features are similar to our own.

❯ Offline events from online sites. In-person mixers and singles events are often incorporated into technology now. The ability to meet with members of a dating site in your area bridges the gap from email to off-screen connecting.

❯ Virtual speed-dating. Taking speed dating to the Web, these sites use webcams and a fast-paced, real-time environment to let you scroll through matches with video-enabled pages.

❯ Calling cards. Reverse-engineering for online dating, these sites create calling cards, which you can discreetly slip to someone you're interested in while you're out living your everyday life, encouraging the stranger to check you out online. When people log in to the site, they can contact you in a safe way if the interest is mutual.

> **Social-media-inspired layout.** As society becomes comfortable with updating statuses, uploading photos with funky filters, and checking in everywhere we go, these sites create different ways to connect with matches by giving you a layout that feels less like email and more like Facebook.

Although newism technology hasn't been tested for years, these sites often see more engagement from users. Nerve.com, a site that was originally founded in 1997 but completely revamped and relaunched in 2011, finds a big difference between users' behavior with traditional tech versus pop-tech. While the revamped site allows you to view a member's profile and send a message as most sites do, the new layout also allows you to reply directly to "shares" (similar to Facebook status updates) for specific questions, such as "What did you do last night?" Research shows that users are 44 percent more likely to receive a response if they write to someone based on a "share" than if they had sent a message without context.

Since trends are continually changing, the specifics of the latest pop-tech flirting options can be found in the Resource section at eFlirtExpert.com/loveatfirstclick, so you're always in the know.

EARLY ADOPTER EDUCATION

Technology may be ever changing, but that doesn't mean your preferences are. Being an early adopter is not for everyone but will let you experience pop-tech flirting before it goes main-stream. Let's review the pros and cons to see if you're up for the download.

❭ Your location.

PRO: New dating technology usually takes off in large cities first before a site or app reaches mainstream appeal, since the success of pop-tech flirting is reliant upon critical mass. Emerging technologies are definitely in a single urbanite's favor, where an abundance of users is almost guaranteed.

CON: If you live outside city limits or aren't willing to date someone who lives in a metropolis, these technologies probably won't apply to you until they've become more widespread.

❭ Flirting potential.

PRO: Big sites can't usually experiment with features the way startups can, so the experience you'll get will be incredibly unique. And they have the agility to pivot quickly when things aren't working for their members. Users are typically more active on the site and more inclined to respond to a message they see.

CON: Since startups don't have the draw of large sites, flirting potential may be slim pickings until they become more popular in your area.

❭ Flexibility.

PRO: New technology can constantly be at your fingertips. Since developments are in flux, you often get a lot of input on a product during the early stages, shaping the digital dating tool into what works best for you. Unlike with big sites, you won't have to worry about whether your feedback is being heard. It's also likely that companies, regardless of size, will release new features to you first.

CON: Being on a new platform will mean spending some time adjusting to the new way of cyber-relating. And all technology might not be fully thought out before the launch, so you might experience more bugs than you're used to.

> **Competition.**

PRO: When one innovative dating site launches, you can bet that similar ones aren't far behind. Competition in the space means that you always have options for where you spend your time, particularly when you determine an affinity for one particular kind of eFlirting.

CON: With competition comes more fragmentation of matches; people who are interested in connecting through one type of approach often end up scattered on other similar sites.

The best thing about early adopter-hood is the opportunity to play. My client Brett is a tech addict, and since he was coding his first program at ten years old, it's not surprising that his iPhone has become his dating and social playground. Obviously, he's pretty comfortable navigating new digital tools, but even if you're not on Brett's level, he teaches a valuable lesson: it's all about exploration. Getting outside your tech comfort zone every once in a while is OK. Just as you might enjoy trying a different cuisine or activity, joining a different site can prove to be a great new experience.

But there are some particulars to look out for when you log in. Here are tips for getting the most out of being an initial user in the Winkisphere:

> **Join ASAP.** Just about every site, app, and social network is worth joining as soon as you hear about it. Frequently, early adopters are given preferential treatment in the form of complimentary or discounted membership—often for the lifetime of your username. There aren't many negatives about a free subscription! With perks like this, you can also expect users to be more engaged near launch and around major media announcements. So if you read about a new site or app through a source like HuffingtonPost.com, click the site's Subscribe button immediately, and get flirting.

> **Engage.** While membership perks are nice, remember that you're there to meet people. Browse through users, communicate with the ones you like, and head out on dates. There may not be hundreds of people who fit your criteria, but it's worth exploring to see if there's One.

> **Return.** New brands that do well spend time and dollars altering their user experience. Through tech evolution and user preferences, they learn how to enhance and add features to keep people wanting more. If you joined a site in the beginning and stopped visiting because traffic to your profile slowed down, it's always worth returning to view new members and the site's changes a few months later.

Mobile Mating

The chronic conundrum of dating online is smoothing the transition from online to offline. Since the nearest intersection of digital dating and in-person interactions is a mobile application, this is the latest growing frontier for helping singles over-come those connection challenges.

Most online dating sites have mobile apps that let you use most of the site's functionality on the go. These are always worth a download so you can be better connected to the matches you're communicating with.

eFlirt Byte: More than 40 percent of
subscribers log on to Match.com through
their mobile devices every month.

And some dating sites give mobile users app-exclusive func-tions. For example, the HowAboutWe app connects to the Foursquare API, making it simple to search for date spots in your vicinity.

LOCATION-BASED LOVE

The popularity of location-based mobile dating apps—technology that allows you to find and meet matches nearby—is growing rapidly and the numbers reflect that:

MeetMoi, a social introduction app that auto-intros you to new matches while you go about your day, launched in 2007 and now has more than 3 million users worldwide.

Grindr, a gay mobile dating app that launched in 2009, now has more than 4 million users. At any given moment, there are as many as 71,000 users logged in. The company also launched *Blendr,* its counterpart for straight singles. Mobile singles are highly engaged users: 96 percent of female users and 93 percent of male members are using the chat feature.

Badoo is a social network centered around meeting new peo-ple rather than connecting with acquaintances. In fact, 68 percent of their signups happen via mobile versus Web, and once users are logged in, they chat with six to ten people per month.

You'll notice that while most of these companies have online URLs, their business is really centered around mobile. Some of the major online dating players are beginning to add location-based technology to their apps, like OkCupid's Locals feature, which works similarly. But since apps are a completely different kind of technology, it's OK to trust those that make it the center of their business, as Badoo does.

APP-PROPRIATE

As with dating sites, each location-based flirting app functions a little differently, but they all allow you to find singles in your vicinity and chat with one another. And if all goes well, it's even easier to meet up for a quick offline interaction. But there are a few things to note when you're flirting via dating apps.

› Your profile is different. While your profile is still your first impression, your match is viewing your digital self on a much smaller screen. So your profile's impact has to pack a bigger punch to get others to message you. Keep your text short, without violating any of the dating-profile principles. On apps, small bites of information that give a range of sides to your personality work best. For inspiration, here's my personal profile on Badoo: "Always wearing heels. Woman in tech. Addicted to chai tea lattes. Cocktail-ring hoarder. Compulsive early adopter. First-time author. Yogi attempting balance."

› Answer every question. With little space to talk about yourself, make sure that you fill out all of the multiple-choice questions that the app asks. Your preferences about children, movies, and smoking will be viewed more frequently than they might on a dating site, since there's a limited amount of information about you available.

> **Messaging isn't texting.** As in online dating, you approach someone through a flirting app with a message. To make it mobile-friendly, the message looks like a text, but you should still treat it as a mini-version of a dating site email: mention a commonality, and ask a question. Two sentences usually do the trick; it's neither too short nor too long for a textlike window. With fewer characters, it's even more important to skip generic sentences to make yourself stand out.

> **Know when to shut down.** Most apps will keep you logged on constantly by default. But when you're browsing the grocery-store aisles in your Sunday housecleaning garb, it's probably not the ideal time to meet an eBachelor or eBachelorette. Make it a habit to log in only when you're ready to flirt and to log out once your eFlirting mission is complete.

> **Never approach without consent.** If you're communicating via the app with a hottie and recognize him or her in the flesh, keep mum. Say hi face-to-face only after you've mutually decided to meet. Otherwise, it comes off as creepy, even if the run-in was by chance.

THE FIRST APP MEETING

When you meet off the screen, you should treat your match like someone who approached you at a bar. In fact, meeting from a dating site and an app are completely different experiences. On apps, spontaneity abounds and is encouraged. Since there's typically much less information exchanged via profiles and messages on apps, it's a lower-pressure way of meeting new people.

Because of this, you can plan on spending even less time together than during a typical first meeting from a traditional online dating site. Think of your match as someone you came across randomly at a coffee shop or a bar, since the level of "getting to know you" is similar. When you're making quick decisions to meet your match, it's even more important to follow the safety guidelines in chapter 6.

Whether you click or not, it's assumed that you won't spend a significant amount of time together. So if you (or your match) want to part ways after twenty minutes, don't be discouraged—this is normal. And actually, if you linger for much longer when you both seem preoccupied, you run the risk of making things awkward for everyone. Just keep in touch, and plan a real date for later in the week.

My client Daryl was complaining that all of the guys on Grindr are just looking to hook up. He lamented that while no-strings-attached relationships can be par for the course in the gay community, he gets frustrated when that's all that's available. But once we started chatting about how he's using the app, I diagnosed his issue: he was logging on only after eleven P.M. on the weekends, when hookups happen. Once he began using the app in the daytime, his experiences changed completely.

Time of day often plays into the success or demise of app relationships. Take your intention into account before reaching out, and make sure that it syncs up with the hour on your watch (or smartphone).

eFlirt Byte: MeetMoi sees the most user activity
on Wednesdays from six to seven P.M. Eastern.

Social Media Flirting

As our lives have become more entwined with social media, it's become an increasingly popular way to meet mates. In fact, I met my hubby-to-be via Twitter. In the beginning of my business, I was cruisin' the Twitterverse to connect with industry experts and wired-in singles. But when I clicked on @URwingman, I swooned. Thomas is a fellow dating coach with a different focus. He's the founder of The Professional Wingman and helps people master the art of offline flirting, approaching, and relationship building. But I'm not talking pickup artist; his style is more about confidence and social savvy. I got lost in the eyes of his avatar staring back at me, but more important, I found his words of wisdom woo-worthy. And the first time I retweeted something brilliant that Thomas said, I was thrilled when he responded.

We bantered for a bit, and then it died down, but I knew it wouldn't be our final 140 characters. Although he lived in Boston and I lived in New York, I sent him a private Direct Message before I headed to Massachusetts to visit my parents. Chatting in a cloud space for just the two of us allowed me to ask him out for a drink without being virtually exposed.

As you've already learned, digital flirting often means abandoning conventional rules. I may have asked Thomas out, but I did it under the guise of business to soften the approach. And even though we began a relationship by working together, it was clear from the first moment we locked eyes offline that chemistry existed beyond our desktops. A short time later, we were tweethearts.

When flirting on social networks, the platform's functionality often determines your eCourtship.

Since social networks were created for connecting versus flirting, shift your thought before you hit Enter. Whether you spy your cyber-crush on Facebook or Foursquare, there are some do's and don'ts that are universal when you're building a relationship via social networks.

The eFlirting process even varies based on your current relationship with this person—whether you've met each other in person already or if you only know each other online. First, let's assume that you've never met offline.

> **Friend and follow.** If you're not digitally connected to your match, it will be awfully hard to make a pass at him or her. Make sure you friend, follow, subscribe, or take whatever the social network calls its form of connecting. This isn't just a technique for making your way onto someone's radar—now you have full access to whatever he or she is posting. You can hope that the person will reciprocate the virtual relationship so you can have mutual contact. A personal connection is best even though most sites make some form of their profiles public, as well as the ability to communicate.

> **Real-time relating.** Skipping straight to asking someone out online without first chatting and flirting is the equivalent of grabbing a random stranger in a bar for a make-out session without saying hello first. So jump in on conversations the other person is engaged in when you have something to add, or comment on his or her latest musing. This will lay the groundwork for a relationship and give the person a head's-up that you've taken an interest in what he or she has to say.

> **Digital discovery.** If you're not sure if your crush is single, you'll need to use your cyber-savvy. Pay close attention to uploaded photos, weekend and evening plans, and the person's tone in communication with others. At the end of the day, most people, even if they're in a relationship, will be flattered if your advances turn flirty. But of course, eliminating embarrassment before you make your move is ideal.

> **Make it private.** To amp up your flirting, you'll definitely need to be out of the public eye. Once you've developed some semblance of an eRelationship, shift to private messages. If the site you're on has an IM feature, this transition often doesn't need much explanation other than the fact that you're both online at the same moment. If it's a less real-time space, like Facebook emails, give the transition some thought, and share something a bit more personal, perhaps a link to an article about a topic you've discussed. Just as I suggested meeting with Thomas under the pretext of business, you should connect over something in common if it makes sense.

> **Getting offline.** Just like online dating, social-media relationships turn romantic offline. Make plans with your crush, whether you take a more subtle approach by suggesting an event of mutual interest or send a blatant date invite. Once you're offline, you'll be able to see if sparks fly.

If you *do* already have an offline relationship with your eSuitor—maybe you went to high school together or have hung out at a mutual friend's BBQ—you've likely already taken many of these steps. Social media should then be a tool for you to develop your rapport and show more obvious interest.

Focus on continuing your relationship dynamic in the most real-time way possible (like IM) to keep things moving forward. And don't be afraid to ask him or her out! Since you know each other already, it's not necessary to wait weeks upon weeks to suggest moving offline—getting face-to-face should still be the goal. Try to make plans sans pals so you can determine if a romantic connection exists beyond the Web.

Remember that the best way to connect will always be face-to-face. So if you are in the same circle of friends and have previously exchanged phone numbers, there's no reason to hide behind a computer screen. Moving things to a social networking site rather than just calling or texting is going backward in your relationship.

With so many ways to date digitally and at the rate tech is developing, there might be something completely new launched by the time you venture into pop-tech flirting territory. But remember: character counts, not character count. So get offline, and make love happen beyond the broadband.

CHAPTER 13

Sign-off Etiquette

TAKING YOUR PROFILE DOWN

Hitting the Disable button on your profile can be exciting. It might mean you've met your match! A person who can hold your attention long enough for you to wonder when you should leap to this next step is certainly someone to keep on your speed dial. But before you change the functionality of your dating life, realize that there are stages of logging off that will ensure that you're not making rash decisions.

Let's face it, things don't always go according to plan in matters of the heart. Sometimes it's clear that it's time to take your profile down, because you've had "the talk" with your new eSweetheart. But perhaps you'd like to take it down because your dating calendar is full, and you can't handle any more inbound flirtations. Or you might be seeing someone who isn't exclusive yet, but your budding romance makes you want to focus on him or her alone.

Whatever the case, taking your profile down shouldn't happen dramatically, without first fully thinking through the decision. I see online daters skip virtually to the next page too soon all the time and lose out on love at first click. My client Sam had a few weeks of great dates with Alfredo, and she hit the Delete button without thinking. But when things started to slow with him and they went their separate ways, she was upset that she had to start over completely, new profile and all.

By taking baby steps, you can always decide to turn back and refresh your online dating life at any point along the way.

Options for Ending Your eDating Life

Before you cancel your account, review these three options:

1. Go inactive. Before you even hover over the Deactivate button, just stop logging in. Avoiding your inbox for a while might be all you need to determine if you should move forward with a more lasting log-off or simply keep your profile on pause. This allows you to sample what a more permanent action would feel like. If you're considering removing your profile because of a lucky match, there's no need to worry about your account still being live. In most cases, the match will be able to see that you haven't logged in recently and can read between the lines of your intentions.

2. Hide. Hiding means that your online persona and profile are hidden, but all of your records are kept intact. Your account is only a mouse click away, so if things don't go well, you don't lose all of your dating data. Your profile, photos, saved searches, and anything else you value are there for you if you decide to reactivate. Since your membership is still active, even when you're hidden, make sure you're aware of your subscription's end date.

3. Delete. This is permanent. And I mean really permanent. There's no magical recycling bin from your desktop that can recover your eFlirting details once you make this decision. So it's important to be very sure of yourself (and your offline relationship) before you erase your eDating identity from the site's server.

Nearly all eDaters go through options 1 and 2 before hitting Delete. Even if you're in a fairly new committed relationship, you should disable for a while before you delete . . . just in case.

Tying Up Loose Strings

You might want to give anyone you are messaging a head's-up before you take any action with your profile. If you're logging off because your mind is busy buzzing with multiple dates, give matches you're into your safety email address so you can continue to communicate without having to worry about other traffic in your inbox. Be vague about the reason for taking your profile dark; if someone goes the extra mile and chats you up off the site or makes plans for a date, it will be worth your energy.

If you're now exclusive with someone, it's important to cut off any loose relationships so you can commit completely. But even if you're not exclusive yet, giving your current matches notice is polite—and strategic. If things don't go according to plan, this will leave the door open for you to rekindle those relationships.

Skip exchanging email addresses, and simply bring up the reason you're leaving the site. While it may seem bold to be so honest, it often gives others more respect for you. Don't overexplain—just keep it simple. Here's a message I wrote for Lindsey:

From: pinkcupcakes
Sent: June 13 11:39AM
To: vangone
Subject: RE: Jet Ski Obsessions
Hey Allen,
Glad to hear your weekend went well. The dinner party sounds
like it was a blast!
Recently, I've started seeing someone. Though it's only in the
beginning stages, I want to give it a fair shot sans distractions,
so I'm going to hold off on other dates for now and log off. I'm
bummed we didn't get to meet, because you seem like a great
guy so far, but perhaps our paths will cross again.
Best of luck!
Lindsey

An email of this nature will almost always elicit a response. In
fact, Allen did write back and mentioned that if things didn't
work out, she should feel free to email him again.

But even without this green light, it's OK to send a follow-
up if things don't work out and you return to the site. Just be
sure to keep the message positive and vague about that relationship that turned to ruin. Try something like this:

Hey Allen,
Hope you've been well! This summer has been busy for me,
but who can complain about taking lots of long weekends away?
Just got back from Napa and was in San Diego a few weeks
before that.
Thought I'd reach out now that I'm dating again. Still up for that
glass of wine? Would love to hear the latest with you.
Lindsey

This lets your match know you're back on the market and avoids any awkward conversations about what happened.

For all of the others you're messaging but aren't really into, you can choose either to notify them or virtually vanish. If you're going to give them a head's up, just send a simple notification. If you're not wowed by them now, it's unlikely that you'll want to drop them a message later if things don't go according to plan.

Rather than handing out your contact information to everyone and continuing your conversations via email, be selective. Keeping the dynamic going with too many matches will defeat the purpose.

For the ones you're dating offline, remember that each relationship you've been building is different. Unlike matches you're messaging with, you've spent actual time with these people and have worked toward developing something. Depending on the reason you're shutting down your online dating life, you might either remove them all from your little black eBook or continue to see just a few. Evaluate where you stand with each, and only keep those you'd like to continue to crush on. If you're signing off, there's a reason, so make sure the people you're currently dating fit within it.

Before you get impulsive about cutting yourself off from those you've met offline, start by slowly distancing yourself. Stay in touch via text, but keep a busy calendar for a while so you don't have to commit to a date when things between you could go deeper. Since you've likely had a make-out (or two), you don't want to throw away what you've worked toward unless you're sure things with another match are getting serious or you've decided this person is a definite nay. Keeping your distance now will soften the blow if you end things.

If and when you're ready to walk away, call and give a similar explanation to the one Lindsey gave Allen. Things have gotten a bit more serious with someone recently. You're not sure where it will go, but you want to give it attention by avoiding distractions. Focus on the fact that your feelings are fresh, so it's clear that you weren't dating one person while all along harboring feelings for another.

Determining Your Match's Staying Power

Now that you've cleared space on your heart's hard drive, let's evaluate the staying power of the match that inspired you to hide your online dating profile.

But first off, let's get one thing straight: Pausing or deleting your profile doesn't mean you're exclusive.

Sometimes the decision to take your profile down is yours alone, and that's OK. There's something to be said for stepping away from your iPad and focusing on only one match, even though you haven't solidified whether you're each other's BF or GF yet. Even if you make this decision on your own, it might still be step number one on the way to exclusivity. Before you move forward, make sure that your match is worth it by answering these few questions:

❯ **How long have you been seeing each other?** Needless to say, taking down your profile after only one date is a presumptuous no-no. There is a difference between a bud and the start of a blossom. Focus your energy on having fun with your fab date offline rather than fussing over what's happening with others online. But if it's been more than three weeks, it's OK to let your mind wander to offline relationship territory.

〉 How much time do you spend together? Every relationship moves at a different pace. Some date once a week in the beginning, while others prefer to get hot and heavy sooner, throwing most of their spare moments into the "we time" pile. If you've been dating for a month but have only been out two or three times, it's still too soon to consider removing your profile. For your own peace of mind, keep your options open until you've spent a more significant amount of time together. The minute you dread a date with someone new, it's time to take your profile down.

〉 Is your dynamic strong? How you interact with each other says a lot about where you are today—and where you're headed in the future. If you still feel those first-date-like nerves or are acting more formally than normal, it's not the right time to worry about your dating site status. Once you enter more comfortable territory, you can revisit the topic.

〉 Do your goals coincide? Be realistic about both your short-term and long-term goals and where they intersect with your match's or not. For example, if you hope to have children in a few years but your date can't stomach being around the little ones in the family, your long-term goals are on opposite sides of the world (wide web). But if your short-term goal is to have fun for the summer with a companion and that seems to be his or her main priority, too, you might want to continue dating this match anyway—just don't do it exclusively. If you're into your match, similar long-term goals are required before you take your profile down. But if it's merely the short term that's on your mind, don't feel guilty for leaving your profile live.

› Have you slept together? Let's face it, getting intimate brings your relationship to a whole new level. For some, this requires taking your profile down, while others are OK with still seeing other people. Either way, it means that your relationship has taken on a new level of priority, at least in the bedroom. Consider what this means to you, and notice if your match's behavior shifts. For example, if he or she wants to spend more time together, you may be headed for exclusivity, while those who act more detached may be signaling that they want to keep it casual. If you want to have the exclusive on your match's booty, make sure that you wait a date or two to bring it up so you don't seem clingy.

› Have you met their peeps? Meeting friends—and, in some cases, family—ups the ante. It's a well-known fact that meeting loved ones is a good sign if you're looking for a more serious relationship. But in the world of Internet dates, it's also a sign that you should give some thought to taking your profile down.

› Are you still daydreaming? If you're letting your mind wander to your match, that's a good sign. A lot of that, and it might be time for you to think about halting the other dates in your life. But if you're stuck contemplating what might happen with other potentials in your queue, you shouldn't give taking your profile down another thought.

If you've decided it's time to take your account down, that doesn't mean that the same is expected of your match. If you're doing it early on—after a few dates or weeks—it's OK to bring it up in discussion if you feel things are going in a good direction. But don't require that your match do the same unless you're an official couple.

Reciprocation is required if you're in a relationship.
Being in a relationship means you've discussed being in one, not merely fallen into comfort with each other. So if you're clearly committed—discussed and everything—take down your profile, and it's OK to recommend that your new honey take down his or her profile, too, if it's still live.

Having "the talk" should be eased into. Gone are the days of sneaking your crush a scrap of paper in history class with yes/no checkboxes. Although technology was the way your flirtations began, something as serious as your relationship status is deserving of a face-to-face conversation. But you can use technology as a *topic* to jumpstart the conversation. Bring up your own profile and the fact that you were thinking of taking a break. Make it a statement, and don't expand until you get a reaction. This will allow you to broach the topic in a casual way and take the discussion wherever it leads. A statement like "I was thinking of taking down my profile" lets your match know where you stand without being too forceful about it. If he or she seems to panic a bit, you can take the conversation down a notch and blame it on something else, like you haven't logged in for a while or you've been busy with work, without needing to profess your undying lust. But if your match seems to be in sync, you can use the topic as a launching pad for discussing your relationship more broadly.

Between "Single" and "In a Relationship"

Of course, your online dating profiles aren't the only sites you have to worry about. Taking down your digital dating persona is the first step, but that doesn't automatically mean that your new boo is ready to go Facebook Official (FBO) and announce you to his or her digital social planet.

If you're new to exclusivity, remove your relationship status from your profile until you're comfortable breaking the news digitally. Going FBO is exciting and usually comes with a virtual outcry of "likes." It's also a big announcement, since for many users, their family and closest friends will potentially see it. And having to switch back to "single" a month later won't go unnoticed. Sure, you can delete the post, erasing your relationship from your timeline, but soon enough, some pals will catch on, which can get uncomfortable when they ask about it on your public page. Trust me, it happens.

Wait until your relationship takes on a more serious tone and the L-bomb is dropped. Professing l-o-v-e to each other is the perfect time to make it online-official. Until then, here are some things to consider before you and your match do.

GOING FACEBOOK OFFICIAL (FBO)

› **Going halfsies.** Although your other half might not be comfortable changing his or her status, that shouldn't stop you, as long as you've discussed that you're BF and GF. Once it's official in your heart, go ahead and make the switch without tagging your boo. Just be aware that you'll inevitably get a few comments from pals asking you who it is. Give your partner a head's up that you'll be adding this to your page.

> **Daily use.** Social platforms have different purposes. Beyond differences between a more professional network like LinkedIn and a more friend-oriented one like Facebook, people also use them in different ways. Some people are on social networks to engage with everybody in their lives, while others have profiles simply to connect with long-lost colleagues and friends. Others use social networking for personal branding or as a research tool. So even if you're ready to announce your status, think twice before you go making ultimatums that might risk your new status—"Accept my relationship request, or else!" Take stock of how your eSweetheart seems to be using the platforms in question.

> **Serious scale.** Even if your BF or GF is a Facebook-aholic, it's unlikely that he or she will want to change the relationship status right away. It has nothing to do with wanting to remain single and more to do with being unsure of making a public announcement and the ramifications if things don't work out. So until you've been happy-go-lucky for a few months post-talk, keep your online-status discussions at bay.

> **Current status.** Even when times get tough, be sure to avoid tongue-in-cheek references to your relationship status, like "It's complicated." They proclaim to the world that you're not living in bliss. Although you may be acting sarcastic, not everyone who comes across your profile will know you well enough to read it that way. Instead, it looks as if you're airing your dirty laundry.

> **Privacy preferences.** Everyone's feelings about the amount of personal information that is publicly available are different. If

your match declines your request to tag him or her, don't take it personally. As long as your other half's status isn't still listed as "single," your relationship is in the clear.

If you think it's complicated to have "the talk" with your soon-to-be honey, don't fret. It doesn't have to be as painful (or scary) as you think. In fact, the relationship chat between my client Tyler and his lady went so well that they decided to have their own unplugging party to celebrate. They pulled out their laptops, logged on to Amor.com, and deleted their accounts at the same moment. A few months later, I even saw pictures that she tagged in a Facebook album of her visiting his family for the first time. Talk about commitment! Removing your profile can be a big deal, so being able to say "Cheers" to your blossoming relationship over a glass of wine and one final log-out is a fun way to celebrate. Congrats!

CHAPTER 14

Tech Woo

BEING A 2.0 COUPLE

It's no secret that good communication is a must in every successful relationship. For most, this conjures up images of date nights, deep conversations, and discussions of compromise. But in our increasingly webby world, good communication doesn't just happen offline; it can come by way of email notifications, wall posts, and text messages, too. This is how we connect with the people in life—our BFFs, bosses, and brothers—and that should extend to your romantic relationship, too, once you meet your right click.

In fact, if you aren't communicating in the cloud with your honey, you're missing out on a valuable part of the modern love dynamic. It will expand the way you relate to each other and add a fourth dimension to your already 3D relationship.

For Thomas and me, two years of digital flirtations, real-life romance, long-distance Skyping, date nights, and sweet-tweet nothings led @URwingman to propose to @eFlirtExpert. But you don't have to be long-distance like we were to integrate tech into the day-to-day of your couple-dom. In today's world, flirting with your partner should happen in person and online.

Take it from a Professional Wingman and an eFlirt Expert who just happen to be tying the knot: continuing to eFlirt with each other is the next gen of relationship dynamics.

Keystrokes Are Sexy

Even though you and your click mate have signed off from online dating, don't ditch the tech altogether—keystrokes can be sexy! Rather than considering it a mere information exchange, as you do with your pals, inject romance into your 2.0 behavior by using these tips on how to take average technology and make it love-appropriate.

TEXTING

Most couples text to keep each other in the loop about their days, plans, and work complaints (without the chance that their boss's prying ears will overhear).

> eFlirt Byte: A study by Zoosk,
> the romantic social network, found that
> 81 percent of couples use technology to interact
> with one another throughout the day.

But forget about the mundane; texting can also be used to develop your relationship. Thomas and I often use it as a way to send sweet nothings to each other.

My favorite text from him was sent on our one-month anniversary. I was in New York, and he was in Boston. He stopped by the gourmet pizza restaurant where we had our first date, ordered our favorite pie, and snapped a photo to send to me.

This was a unique way to say Happy Anniversary and tell me that he was craving *us*.

Now, not *every* message needs to be this personal. Any behavior on overload will begin to desensitize your partner. But giving your text messages a sweeter touch from time to time will show your partner that he or she is special in a new way.

VIDEO

Distance makes the heart grow fonder. While it sounds like a cliché, I learned that it's true while dating Thomas. Skype dates were our favorite form of tech communication: we'd dress up for date night, light candles, pour wine, and play twenty questions. There's something about still wanting to make each other swoon from a distance that can reignite the most connected relationships.

Even if your honey is only on a business trip for a few nights, viewing each other over video will add a new dimension to your relationship. Having a screen between the two of you often will make you more willing to share your feelings because you're forced to emote through words rather than actions.

ECARDS

Sending paper cards never goes out of style, but Thomas and I are also huge fans of sending virtual cards. Whether it's something funny, sassy, or sweet, it's nice to know that your boo is thinking of you even if it's only a workday that's keeping you apart.

Skip the more formal thank-you versions, and go for humorous or heartwarming ones. It's even better when the personality of the eCard fits the vibe of your relationship. Thomas is oddly obsessed with PB&J sandwiches, and a big part of our couple dynamic is being silly together. So on National PB&J Day, I sent him an eCard celebrating the holiday (which he wasn't aware of) and told him that I loved him more than he loved the sandwich (which is a *lot!*). Sending a card for something a little off-the-wall got his attention and made my sweetie smile.

APPS

It can be fun to play games together device-to-device. But beyond Words With Friends, there are many apps that can support your romantic life, like restaurant-rating resources for date night, daily deal alerts for activities to opt into together, and travel apps for spur-of-the-moment trips.

When looking for new apps to download for love, Thomas and I consider adventure, convenience, and thoughtfulness. In your mobile toolbox, you want to have apps that will help create an offline experience for you both. You can find our personal list of must-downloads at eFlirtExpert.com/loveatfirstclick.

SOCIAL MEDIA

If you're active on social media platforms, you should at a minimum be tagging your partner in posts when you mention him or her. But connecting beyond your wall or stream will bring you closer online and offline. Here are some tips for booting up your love life via social media:

> **Post as a pair.** Thomas and I love to tweet each other even when we're hanging nearby. Sharing a picture of our picnic in the park as we check in on Foursquare, along with a blissful comment, is a public proclamation of gratitude. If your significant other is into social media the way Thomas and I are, opting in together will

make the otherwise solitary online act a shared experience. But it also works well if your partner isn't into social sharing. Doing it together will become a tender gesture rather than a potential annoyance that you're posting about him or her solo.

> **Cheer each other up.** Perhaps the best feeling I get from social media with my man is when I'm having a rough day and Thomas tweets how special I am. You don't need to make it publicly known that you're going through something; just share your candid thoughts on how awesome he or she is. Trust me, it will make your mate's heart skip a byte.

> **Create together.** Experiencing certain parts of social networks together inspires a common digital adventure. Develop something specific that you can both add to, like a Facebook photo album or a Pinterest mood board. You can sit and do this together or work on it when you're apart so your partner has something interesting to smile at the next time he or she logs in.

> **Ping each other's inbox.** Although most of social media is public, don't forget that fun can happen behind virtual doors, too. I often send Thomas songs via Spotify during the day. They pop up in his private inbox with a note that's either an explanation of why the song is perfect for us or a lyric that touched my heart. Never underestimate the value of keeping things private by sending him or her a link in a DM on Twitter or a message about a Facebook Connect app for couples.

But some things are just too private to make public. On Zoosk, you can create a couple's profile. It's just like a digital scrapbook: you post photos of your recent vacations or recipes from your tandem cooking experiments. It provides a continuation of online dating, where you can flirt in one place either entirely privately or in a more contained network space. Thomas and I not only use it to keep a record of our own relationship, but we also reserve it for chitchat that single friends wouldn't be interested in but couple friends adore.

eFlirt Byte: Zoosk found that
60 percent of Americans say they are cautious
about posting romantic posts on social media
because they are worried about what
their coworkers might think.

Online Glitches

Just because you met on the Internet doesn't mean that you'll never have online issues with each other. In fact, having more access to relationship temptations like exes on Facebook and casual encounters on Craigslist means that trust for your partner needs to extend to the Web. Tech can add a new element to your love life, but it can also injure it beyond repair.

eFlirt Byte: A survey by the American
Academy of Matrimonial Lawyers found that
66 percent of U.S. marriages cite Facebook
as the reason for divorce.

When there's a screen between you, it's easy to let a conversation with an old flame or a Facebook "friend" get too explicit and be the demise of your current relationship. To combat this, some couples have an open-password relationship so they can access each other's digital lives—from personal email addresses to Twitter accounts—whenever they desire. But this level of sharing isn't a comfortable option for all lovebirds. Some consider it oversharing, and others don't see the need.

Being doubt-free about your honey's browser history won't happen if you don't have trust in the other aspects of life. And even then, open communication about your Web behavior should be a priority for the length of your relationship. Confidence in the path your relationship is taking combined with the knowledge of each other's online relationships will strengthen your partnership.

To make sure that tech doesn't get in the way of your love connection, follow these guidelines:

> **Go tech commando.** Frequently spending time together sans devices will allow you to focus only on your bond with each other. Whether it's a few hours a week when phones aren't allowed or a cell-free zone in the house, like your bedroom, shutting down from time to time will ensure that tech never becomes a crutch.

> **Respect your relationship.** Announcing your relationship troubles on the Web will only make them more challenging to overcome. Avoid spiteful acts that attempt to undermine your partner, and keep your personal issues off Facebook.

> **Avoid temptation.** If things are getting a little inappropriate with someone online, distance yourself by turning off IM features and taking more time to respond. And if the person doesn't take the hint, unfriend him or her altogether.

❯ Be transparent. Talking about online issues with your honey will encourage trust. So if an ex just friended or followed you and you're not sure what to think of it, bring it up casually with your partner. Your mate will appreciate that you want to talk it through together. This may be less comfortable for men, who are known for handling situations on their own, but broaching the topic sooner rather than later is even more important for them. If you don't disclose the information and your honey finds out, he or she may think you have something to hide when you don't.

❯ Make decisions together. Decide together what news to disclose about your relationship online. Even though you're together, it's still important to be sensitive about you and your partner's more personal moments. Some couples have general rules—like if it involves children, it's off limits—or you can take it on a case-by-case basis. For example, if your significant other just got laid off, don't go tweeting about it before discussing it together.

❯ Know when to shut down. Notifications should not interrupt intimate moments. When your clothes come off, put the phone away! While it may sound ridiculous to have to include this rule, a study by Retrevo, a website that reviews consumer electronics, suggested some interesting bedroom behavior: about one in ten people younger than twenty-five wouldn't mind being interrupted by an electronic message during sex, and 6 percent older than twenty-five said they'd be OK with it. When you're in a relationship, you may be comfortable with your partner, but you should never be this blasé. If your phone rings or pings mid-moment, ignore it.

Although these guidelines may seem to be built for digital defense against creating potential problems in your relationship, best practices will also help when good things enter your life. When Thomas and I got engaged, we made the decision to wait to announce it on the Web until we had the chance to tell all of our close friends and family individually (and in person when possible). And because we're a little sappy and techie, we also decided to each write a blog post about the experience as part of the announcement. Discussing this beforehand made being on the same page for going FBO as "engaged" a simple step. In fact, the hardest part was keeping our cousins from tagging us in their excitement when we told them face-to-face.

Fixing Your Fails

Some common relationship challenges can be solved with an injection of tech. And no, I'm not just talking about tapping open the 1800Flowers app! Relationship issues should always start with mutual awareness and discussion. But once you voice the struggles you're having to your significant other through face-to-face communication, technology can play a part in the solution via eCommunication. Whether you're growing apart or are bored and restless, I've got your digital solutions to avoiding relationship ruin.

> **If you've grown complacent.** Being lazy in your couple-dom risks your mate feeling unappreciated. But being more proactive by planning date excursions is something that many apps can solve. Depending on your interests, you can download solutions ranging from city guides to on-the-spot deals. For a premium

experience, log into Couples.HowAboutWe.com, which makes discovering, purchasing, planning, and redeeming amazing date ideas no-nonsense for you but adds mega-wow factor for your honey.

> **If you've grown apart.** When you just don't get each other anymore, reconnecting is needed. Get back on the same page by opening a new one on the Web: download a twenty-questions app, take the Myers-Briggs test together online, or enjoy a class online together to develop a new hobby. You can also reminisce about how you met to get the spark back. Opt into eHarmony's Facebook app, The Story of Us; when you enter the date you met, the app will auto-populate photos to create a relationship timeline. Then, you can sit together and add memories from other milestones like your first kiss.

> **If you forget the little things.** While small mishaps might not seem like an issue at the time, they can add up to be a big deal later. Reminders on mobile to-do lists solve the age-old problem of forgetting to bring home the milk. Tech can take you the extra mile and schedule recurring surprises like champagne deliveries, too.

> **If you're bored.** Even when your heart is on solid ground, your day-to-day with each other can get monotonous. Break out of the relationship rut by creating special occasions. With cyber-help, it's not even necessary to leave home. Thomas's and my favorite way to remind ourselves that we're special is to have stay-dates. Dressed up with wine and candles, we slow-dance in our apartment to the online playlist he curated just for me.

⟩ If your attraction wanes. Sometimes the spark dies down in the bedroom. But beyond vibrators, tech can get your blood pumping again, too. When libidos are low, focus first on endorphins, which can boost your sex drive. Try a fitness app together that will make working out fun and create a little competition. And then download apps to get you in the mood, such as sexy game apps that will take Spin the Bottle to an adult level.

Just as knowing how to boot up and embrace digitally is important, so is realizing when it's time to shut down. Technology should be used to enhance your relationship, never to hinder it. Be sure that you're never hiding behind a screen, and use it instead only as a tool to make you and your mate more blissful in real time. When date night comes, put all devices away. Your relationship face-to-face is much more important than anything technology can display. Whether you've been with your honey for five days or fifty years, focus entirely on the love glowing bright.

Afterword
YOUR LAST CLICK

Maybe you've been online dating for eight years. Or perhaps it's only been eight *minutes*. Either way, love is only a click away. In fact, you might be hovering over your lifetime mate right now. But without taking action, you won't know.

Explore. Date. Search. Glow. Click. Crush. Text. Fall. And log off.

You know the ins and outs now: what makes a great profile clickable, the nuances of finding your eMister or eMissus, and how to juggle dates better than any character in a rom-com.

Don't forget that in the Wink Wide Web, the little things matter most. Although it may seem insignificant to revise a few sentences in your profile, it will have a huge impact. Not only will it attract new matches, but it will also send you straight to the top of the search results, encouraging new traffic. Editing your search criteria takes only a moment, but it means you'll see new keyboard cuties, one of whom could be a lasting love. Hugging a match when you first meet could mean developing chemistry throughout the evening instead of thinking he or she wasn't your right click.

But when you're connecting wire-to-wire, don't lose sight of you, compromise too much, or get caught up in "strategizing."

Sometimes things get too black-and-white when your dating life is on-screen, so don't be afraid to inject spontaneity and try new things. Meet up with a match you might otherwise pass over, IM and head out on a date the same night, and take chances. Love doesn't exist without risk.

Regardless of where you are physically or virtually, love *will* find its way to you. Whether you reach for the same pint of Ben & Jerry's in the freezer section, spot someone while searching on Chemistry.com, or connect through a Facebook friend, you need to trust your heart. What it tells you should trump everything. I always tell my clients that they'll know they've met their click mate when someone makes them want to break all the rules. Remember that while eFlirting has a formula, your heart has the final solution. No rules are hard and fast where love is concerned.

For Thomas and me, it was love at first click. But he wasn't my first virtual match. I had been waiting for the page to load with my eRomeo for years. Logging on has led me and so many of my clients to lasting love. Now that you're eFlirting-informed, I hope you click on happily ever after, too.

Acknowledgments

I'm honestly not sure how to put gratitude into words for an experience that has truly left me speechless. My amazing parents, Rob and Lorraine Davis, have encouraged every creative moment of my life. From pink and blue kindergarten finger paintings to shakin' my booty during jazz-dance solos, from jotting down poetry homework assignments to scripting my first book, you've always embraced what's made me unique. Thank you for never batting an eyelash at my ideas, allowing me to live an innovative life, and showing me that the path less traveled is always worth it. Without your life lessons, I would have never had the courage and confidence to compose the entirety of this book.

It was Kirsten Neuhaus, the ultimate publishing matchmaker, who helped me find literary love at Atria Books. You are so much more to me than a simple negotiator of book deals. Thank you for listening to every freak-out call, doling out each word of wisdom, and helping me take my book from its first baby steps to adulthood. We wouldn't have met without Lou Caravella, my longtime PR and marketing manager extraordinaire. Throughout this experience, you constantly pushed me—

and this book—forward. I'm grateful to you for not only your edits, comments, and feedback but, more important, for giving me much-needed perspective.

Amy Tannenbaum, my editor, has exceeded every definition of her role that I could find. Thank you for believing in me before we even had our first date. You made my advice shine on the page. I trust you with my every word, acronym (even IRL), and exclamation point! From our proposal courtship till now, I can't imagine being exclusive with anyone else. And our lettered love fest wouldn't be complete without my publisher, Judith Curr. I'm honored to be an Atria Books author and appreciate your dedication to the decisions that you knew would make my book its best. Special thanks to everyone at Atria who touched this author's heart and pages, especially Alysha Bullock, Diana Franco, Julie Schroeder, Julia Scribner, and Kyoko Watanabe.

Shout out to my Copy Cuties: Paola Hernandez, Samantha Eng, and Kristin Manganello. Through researching, editing, reading, and rereading, you made sure all my i's were dotted and all my t's were crossed. I bow down to your #eFlirtPower! I send special love to Jess Hartman, the first Certified eFlirter. You've been my anchor every step of the way.

Few people on my team have seen the intricacies of my journey through author-dom quite the way Krissy Dolor has. Sitting next to me day in and day out, brainstorming every headline, listening to my every overexplained concept, editing each chapter at sunrise, supporting our clients as I wrote—you are truly my Jill of All Trades. Whenever I was wrist-weary, you were the muscle that held my writing world together.

I wouldn't have survived without Stephanie Frerich, either. You motivated me. You filled me in. You gave it to me straight as no one else could. Whether you're acting as my creative advisor or my publishing educator, you are most certainly my secret weapon.

Thanks to my little brother and sister, Robbie and Lindsey Davis, for keeping me laughing. You remind me that big milestones can't always be thought of so seriously. I needed every tweet, text, and status update that we exchanged. Love you both.

Hugs to my girls: Sarah Kiernan, Gretchen Hartig, Stacy Mafera, Kelli MacKay, Amber Rae, and Alexa Scordato. Thank you for letting me blow up your iPhones and crash at your homes. Whether I was celebrating or crying, you were always cheering me on.

Michelle Kinney Photography, you make me look gorg every time. Thanks for the amazing author photo on the back cover and for truly capturing the Real-Time Me on camera.

Facebook and Twitter followers, you rock my world! Thank you *all* for your overwhelming enthusiasm and everyday excitement for this book. A special shout-out to those who won the Facebook character crowdsource naming contests: April Obey, Kerri Majewski Dunne, Erin Scottberg, Douglas Paul, Dennis Kisyk, Bruce Bernstein, Melissa Mae, Kelli Powers, Nikki Robinson, Tereza Nemessanyi, Stacey Lynne, Richard James, Ross Felix, Katie Morse, Lucinda Hark, and Amanda Bissel.

I'm thankful to my many clients for their daily inspiration. Your successes and struggles are my own and affect my writing far beyond storytelling. Your experiences have encouraged troubleshooting tips and purposeful pondering and allow everyone who reads this book to realize that he or she is not alone.

And to my own true-life testimonial and fiancé, Thomas Edwards, you've been there for me in so many ways, whether you're making sure I take care of my carpal tunnel (hawk!) or simply holding my heart. I know this has been a writing whirlwind, but your support and love are all I've ever needed.

Thank you, everyone, for making sure I left my heart on the book binding. xo